Michele Emmer

Mathland
From Flatland to Hypersurfaces

Foreword by Antonino Saggio

Translation into English by Stephen Jackson

A CIP catalogue record for this book is available from the Library of Congress, Washington D.C., USA.

Deutsche Bibliothek Cataloging-in-Publication Data

Bibliographic information published by Die Deutsche Bibliothek
Die Deutsche Bibliothek lists this publication in the Deutsche Nationalbibliografie; detailed bibliographic data is available in the Internet at <http://dnb.ddb.de>.

Original edition:
Mathlandia (Universale di Architettura 142, collana fondata da Bruno Zevi; La Rivoluzione Informatica, sezione a cura di Antonino Saggio).
© 2004 Testo & Immagine, Turin

© 2004 Birkhäuser – Publishers for Architecture, P.O. Box 133, CH-4010 Basel, Switzerland.
Part of Springer Science+Business Media Publishing Group.
Printed on acid-free paper produced from chlorine-free pulp. TCF ∞
Printed in Italy
ISBN 3-7643-0149-X

9 8 7 6 5 4 3 2 1   http://www.birkhauser.ch

Contents

To Marta and Matteo,
architects

All my thanks to Giusi Di Cristina: she suggested to me a few projects of contemporary architects interesting for this book.

Leaps into New Worlds

by Antonino Saggio

Michele Emmer deals with several absolutely crucial arguments in this volume. To recall them in order:

a. space does not exist as an objective fact but simply as a mental (and scientific) form;

b. these mental and scientific forms of representing space vary from era to era (for example flat Euclidean space, three-dimensional Cartesian space, Gauss' curvilinear geometry, Riemann's 'n-dimensional' geometry, etc.);

c. these mental and scientific forms have utilitarian value. We use them if they work, we set them aside if they do not work. Euclidean geometry is more than accurate when dividing up farmland but we must come up with another one to measure the curvature of solar rays. (At times, the truth is mathematicians first invent the scientific theory and then later, occasionally much later, discover the physical phenomena to which it could usefully be applied);

d. these mental forms in any case have, or can have, intrinsic beauty. This aspect of beauty cannot be ignored because otherwise we could not explain either the total immersion the work of the mathematician requires, or the intimate familiarity between mathematician and architecture: even though from different angles, they are both polysemic disciplines, they serve a practical end, but they neither exhaust themselves nor become flat on this.

Setting aside the exceptional competency of the author, these arguments are illustrated in *Mathland* with two rare qualities: first of all, with exemplary clarity and secondly through a controlled, subterranean passion that is still however transmitted to the reader. I believe many, after the first reading, will want to return to the pages to make drawings and notes, to attempt to read more on the same material by the same scholar. I am also convinced that if this book falls into the hands of an intelligent high school student or a student of architecture or engineering that it would be a good way of understanding the great framework in which to apply the necessary hard work of mathematics. But naturally *Mathland* has even greater importance as part of this book series for architects and researchers who give center place to the relationship between computer technology, new scientific discoveries and the central problem of architects: space. Emmer writes:

> I would like to recount just a small part of the story that led to profound changes in our idea of the space that surrounds us, and help understand how in some sense we ourselves create and invent space, modifying it according to changes in our ideas of the universe. Or perhaps one could say it is the universe that is modified following the mutations in our theories. The word mutation, the word transformation are the keys to this understanding.

Space, as shown in this book, "mutates" and is strictly dependent on our scientific concepts. The concept of mutation of these scientific concepts is important because even architecture mutates over time with the various periods and variations in the tools that allow its realization. Now, we maintain the fundamental tools that give form to architecture are not only materials, construction techniques and functions but above all spatial and scientific concepts. As if mathematical, geometric and scientific knowledge of space is transformed into physical construction, into "things" through architecture. Look for example at the Egyptian Pyramid. Is not the Pyramid (and I have already discussed this theme in this series) the edification of several notions of geometry and trigonometry? Indeed, without those notions, without those mental forms, would the Pyramid even be conceivable? Is not the Pantheon the fruit of a very sophisticated geometric calculation, of considering space and calculations under the form of a "geometry" evidently possessed by the Romans (who would have never been able to construct that type of edifice with their abstruse numbers). And let us make the example of all examples with the affirmation of a new architecture at the beginning of the 15th century. Was not the invention of perspective perhaps at the basis of the transformation of the architecture of Humanism? Perspective became 'reified'. Indeed, the scientific concept is precisely what finally makes space perceptibly "measurable" and leads us to consider an architecture made in its image and likeness: a modular, proportioned architecture, made up of repeatable elements made to be "perspectiveable".

We can be certain of some of these relationships between the scientific concepts of space and architecture, the relationship between perspective, the architecture of Humanism and the

Ptolemaic universe, or that of Cartesian space, of the Mongian projection system and the progressive birth of an architecture first a-perspective and then more and more abstract and analytical. But what is happening today? Where are we going? Because if the concept of space has been mutated (and how it has!) and if the computer technology of this mutation is an agent to at least two or three different powers, then we are in a field of research as rich as it is difficult.

To understand some of these territories and attitudes, it would be useful to recall one point that moves throughout this book. This is the figure of the leap or rather the act of the leap. Emmer explains that in order to understand a space one cannot be immersed in it but must make a leap outside it. Remember? In another circumstance we spoke of fish: fish only know fluid as if it were air around them. They know nothing either of what the sea or a lake or a river might really be and know even less the space in which humans live. Only a "leap" outside that aquatic surface can open up the sensation of another space.

Now this book has made an indispensable contribution and enriched research into new spaces. We begin to understand the laws and see several possibilities. Above all we are in a "topological" concept of space (we are not interested in the construction of geometric "absolutes" but in systems of families and possible relationships between forms) and are also working to give form in architecture and spaces actually explorable in more dimensions with respect to the three Cartesian ones, dimensions in which the space-time geometry is actually something different than what we have been accustomed to since Newton. How to do that? How to imagine these spaces that are "absolutely" just as real as those we are traditionally accustomed to considering? In reading this book, you will see that asking these questions will seem natural to you as well. Welcome to *Mathland* and just like dolphins that take oxygen to leap out of the sea or like Abbott's Square suddenly catapulted into three dimensions, you will think as well:

"An unspeakable horror seized me. There was a darkness; then a dizzy, sickening sensation of sight that was not like seeing; I saw a Line that was no Line; Space that was not Space: I was myself, and not myself. … Either this is madness or it is Hell." But anguish quickly gave way to wonder: "A new world!"

Introduction: Space is Mathematics

In mathematics lies the essence of the spirit
ROBERT MUSIL

I feel I am perceiving a decline in the belief that in philosophy it is necessary to lean on the opinions of some celebrated author; as if our mind should remain completely sterile and infertile when not mixed with another's discourse; and perhaps it should believe philosophy is a book or the fantasy of man, such as the *Iliad* or *Orlando Furioso*, books in which the least important thing is that what is written is true. But things are not thus. Philosophy is written in this great book that is continuously open in front of our eyes (I mean the universe), but it can not be understood without first learning to understand its language and characters, and what is written. It is written in a mathematical language and the characters are triangles, circles and other geometric figures; without these, it is impossible to humanly understand a word; without these it is mere wandering in vain around a dark maze.

The words of Galileo Galilei written in *Il Saggiatore* (*The Assayer*), published in Rome in 1623. Without mathematical structures, nature cannot be comprehended. Mathematics is the language of nature. Let's skip over several centuries. In 1904 a famous painter wrote to Emile Bernard:

Traiter la nature par le cylindre, la sphère, le cône, le tous mis en perspective, soit que chaque côté d'un objet, d'un plan, se dirige vers un point central. Les lignes parallèles à l'horizon donnent l'étendue, soit une section de la nature. […] Les lignes perpendiculaires à cet horizon donnent le profondeur. Or, la nature, pour nous hommes, est plus en profondeur qu'en surface, d'où la nécessité d'introduire dans nos vibrations de lumière, représentée par les rouges et le jaunes, une somme suffisante de bleutés, pour faire sentir l'air.

In speaking of Cézanne, Lionello Venturi commented that cylinders, spheres and cones were not seen in his paintings. Therefore the phrase expressed an ideal aspiration toward an organization of forms transcending nature, nothing more.

The landscape of geometry from Galileo's era changed during the period when Cézanne was painting, in fact a few years earlier.

P. Cézanne, Still Life with Fruit Dish, *1879-82.*

Geometry changed profoundly during the second half of the 19th century. Between 1830 and 1850, Lobachevsky and Bolyai created the first examples of non-Euclidean geometry, in which Euclid's famous fifth postulate on parallel lines was no longer valid. Not without doubts and disagreements, Lobachevsky would call his geometry (now called hyperbolic non-Euclidean geometry) imaginary geometry; such was its contrast to common sense. Non-Euclidean geometry remained for many years a marginal aspect of geometry, a sort of curiosity, until it was incorporated as an integral part of mathematics through the general concepts of G.F.B. Riemann (1826-1866). In 1854, Riemann presented, before the Faculty of the University of Göttingen, his famous dissertation entitled *Ueber die Hypothesen welche der Geometrie zu Grunde liegen* (*On the Hypotheses at the Basis of Geometry*), not published until 1867. In his presentation, Riemann supported a global vision of geometry as the study of a variety of any number of dimensions in any type of space. According to Riemann's concept, geometry no longer necessarily had to deal with points or space in the ordinary sense but rather a group of ordered *n*-ple coordinates. In 1872, Felix Klein (1849-1925), after becoming professor at Erlangen, in his inaugural speech known as the *Erlangen Program*, described geometry as the study of the property of figures having an invariant character with respect to a particular group of transformations. Consequently, each classification of the groups of transformations became a codification of the different geometries. For example, Euclidean plane geometry is the study of the properties of figures that remain invariant with respect to the group of rigid transformations of the plane formed by translation and rotation. Jules-Henri Poincaré stated:

> Geometric axioms are neither a priori synthetic judgments nor experimental facts. They are conventions; our choice, from among all possible conventions, is guided by experimental facts, but remains free and is not limited by the necessity of avoiding all contradictions. Thus postulates can remain rigorously true, even if experimental laws that have determined their adoption are no more than approximative. In other words, the axioms of geometry are nothing more than disguised definitions. Therefore, it makes no sense to consider the question: "Is Euclidean geometry true?" Just as it makes no sense to ask if the metric system is true or the old systems of measurement are false, or if Cartesian coordinates are true and polar ones false. One geometry cannot be more true than another; it can only be more convenient. Euclidean geometry is, and will remain, the most convenient.

Poincaré will always be attributed with the official creation of that sector of mathematics now called "topology" with his book *Analysis Sitûs*, the Latin translation of a Greek name, published in 1895. "As far as I'm concerned, all the various research in which I have been involved has led to Analysis Situs [literally "Analysis of Position"]." Poincaré defined topology as the science that shows us the qualitative properties of geometric figures not only in ordinary space but also in space with more than three dimensions.

Let us make another leap forward. We are at the end of the 1960s. Benoit Mandelbrot discovers (or invents?) fractals. In 1984, thinking back on the early experiences with fractal geometry, Mandelbrot observed:

Why is geometry frequently described as cold and dry? One reason is its inability to describe the form of a cloud, a mountain, a coast or a tree. Clouds are not spheres, mountains are not cones, coasts are not circles and riverbanks are not regular, not even light travels along a straight line. […] Nature reveals not simply a higher degree of complexity but a completely different level.

Fractal geometry presents itself as the geometry most adapted to studying the complexity of natural forms and their evolution. In an article in *Scientific American* several years ago, some authors of the most beautiful fractal images confirmed that fractal geometry seems to describe the forms and configurations of nature in a way that is not only more succinct but also esthetically more valid with respect to traditional Euclidean geometry; fractals as the language itself of geometry.

This completely obvious attempt to consider fractal geometry as the "one true geometry of nature", the true key that allows reading and understanding natural phenomena, is one of the reasons many scientists became suspicious.

If we add to all this the geometry of complex systems, chaos theory and all the "mathematical" images discovered (or invented) by mathematicians in the past thirty years using computer graphics, we can easily see how mathematics has essentially contributed more than once to changing our idea of space, of the space in which we live and the idea itself of space.

Mathematics is not a mere tool of kitchen recipes, but has contributed to, if not determined, our way of conceiving space on the earth and in the universe. Awareness is lacking of mathematics as an essential tool of our culture. This explains the great delay in our understanding and therefore creating our own ideas from what mathematicians have clarified for decades.

This particularly regards topology, the science of transformations, the science of invariants. See for example the design by Frank O. Gehry for the new Guggenheim Museum in Manhattan, New York; a design even more stimulating, even more *topological*, than the one for the Guggenheim in Bilbao.

Certainly the cultural leap is remarkable; construction using techniques and materials that allow realizing transformation, rendering it almost continuous, a sort of contradiction between the finished construction and its deformation. Naturally, I do not mean

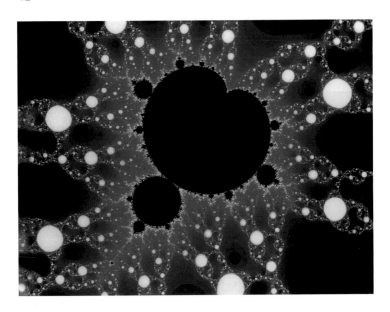

Fractal images (from H.-O. Peitgen, P.H. Richter, The Beauty of Fractals, *Springer, Berlin 1986. Next page: Frank O. Gehry, New Guggenheim Museum, New York, maquettes.*

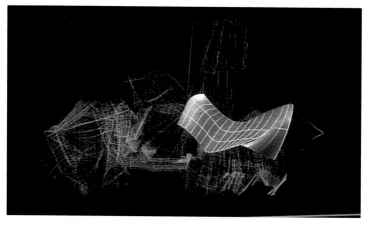

to say that all architects should profoundly study mathematics and topology (even though it would not hurt them) as much as they should be attentive to what happens in the scientific world, recognize the signals to understand what is maturing again in our idea of the world. It is interesting we have also begun to study contemporary architecture by utilizing the tools made available by mathematics and science, cultural tools as well as technical.

I would like to recount just a small part of the story that led to profound changes in our idea of the space that surrounds us, and help understand how in some sense we ourselves create and invent space, modifying it according to changes in our ideas of the universe. Or perhaps one could say it is the universe that is modified following the mutations in our theories. The word "mutation", the word "transformation" are the keys to this understanding.

We will need a guide in this voyage through the idea of space. Our guide should be a character who has, in turn, also made a great voyage, even if only virtual. (And anyway, virtual reality today seems exactly the ideal place for the design of space.) The character in question is the Square, protagonist of the story told by Edwin A. Abbott in the novel *Flatland: A Romance of Many Dimensions*.

As in every good journey, an itinerary must be outlined, an itinerary with all the elements present used to give meaning to the word "space".

– The first element is without the shadow of a doubt the space Euclid defined, with the definitions, axioms and properties of the objects that must exist in this space; the space of perfection, the Platonic space; an idea that spans the centuries of mankind as the matrix and measure of the universe; the mathematics, the geometry that would explain everything, even the forms of living beings. *Curves of Life* was the title of a famous twentieth-century book by Cook who never imagined how true it really was to rediscover mathematical curves in the forms of nature, even those at the origin of life. From the famous 1914 book by D'Arcy Thompson, *On Growth and Form* to the catastrophe theory of René Thom, complexity and the Lorentz effect, and non-linear dynamic systems.

– The second element is freedom; mathematics and geometry seem to be the realm of dryness. Those who have never been involved in mathematics, who have never studied mathematics with interest at school, are not able to understand the deep emotion mathematics can spark. Neither can they understand that mathematics is a highly creative activity. Nor that is a realm of freedom where not only are new objects, new theories, and new fields of research invented (or discovered) but even new problems. Furthermore, since the mathematician has no need for great finan-

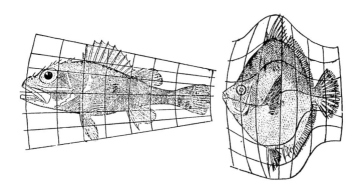

Top: an image of transformation by D'A.W. Thompson, On Growth and Form. *Left: an image of the "Lorentz effect". Right:* The Curves of Life, *by Th.A. Cook.*

cial resources, it could well be said that mathematics is the empire of freedom and fantasy; and certainly of rigor.

This reasoning is very true. The discovery of non-Euclidean geometries and higher dimensions is one of the most interesting examples in part because of the profound repercussions many ideas from mathematicians have had on humanistic culture and art.

– The third element to consider is how all these ideas are transmitted and assimilated, perhaps not completely understood and only overheard by different sectors of society. Architect Alicia Imperiale wrote in the chapter "Digital Technologies and New Surfaces" in the book *New Bidimensionalities*: "Architects freely appropriate specific methodologies from other disciplines. This can be attributed to the fact that broad cultural changes are verified quicker in other contexts than in architecture." She adds:

> Architecture reflects the changes that occur in culture, albeit many feel at a painfully slow pace. […] In constantly seeking to occupy an avant-garde role, architects think the information borrowed from other disciplines can be rapidly assimilated into architectural design. Nevertheless, this 'translatability', the transfer from one language to another, remains a problem. […] Architects more and more frequently look to other disciplines and industrial processes for inspiration, and make ever greater use of computer design and industrial production software originally developed for other sectors.

Later on, Ms. Imperiale recalls, "it is interesting to note that, in the information era, disciplines once distinct are now linked to each other through a universal language: the digital binary code." Does the computer resolve all problems?

– The fourth element is the computer, the graphic computer, the logical and geometric machine par excellence; the concrete idea of an intelligent machine capable of dealing with very different problems as long as we are capable of making it understand the language we use; the ingenious idea of a mathematician, brought to fruition under the stimulus of war; a machine built by man, with a logic inside it that was also built by man, designed by man; a very sophisticated tool, irreplaceable, and not just in architecture; truly a tool indeed.

– The fifth element is progress, the word "progress". Can we speak of progress when considering non-Euclidean geometries, new dimensions, topology and the explosion of geometry and mathematics in the twentieth century? We can definitely speak of knowledge, but not in the sense that new results cancel previous ones. Mathematicians say that "mathematics is like a pig, nothing gets thrown away, sooner or later even those things that seem abstract and even meaningless may become useful". Ms. Imperiale writes, quoting Bernard Cache, that topology is effectively an integral part of the system of Euclidean geometry.

What has escaped the one who wrote these words is what the word "space" means in geometry. Words, exactly. Where instead the changing of geometry serves to deal with problems that are different because the structure of space is different. Space is properties, not the objects it contains. Words.

– The sixth element is words. One of humanity's great capabilities is naming things. Many times in "naming" words are used that are already in current use. This habit at times creates problems because in hearing these words the impression is given of understanding or at least hearing what something is about. That has frequently happened over the past few years in mathematics with words like fractals, catastrophe, complexity and hyperspace; symbolic, metaphorical words. Even topology, dimensionality and seriality at this point make up part of common language, or at least the common language of architects.

To continue, this journey will be made among words, computers, axioms, transformations, words, freedom.

Obviously always keeping mathematics in mind as a reference. Never neglecting, when the occasion arises, to shed light on the links of mathematics with art, literature, images and cinema in order to understand how the principal aspect of mathematics is cultural and intellectual; mathematics not as a mere tool, perhaps to select students in school. Telling a story, the idea of space, digressing not to speak of something else but seeking to give a framework to the culture of an era, the culture of which architecture is an important part. To understand, to do, aspiring to inform and to somewhat fascinate.

1. The Beginning: from Euclid to The Death Star

In the first film from the *Star Wars* series, who does not remember the sequence where Skywalker's spaceship must penetrate the enormous space station, the "Death Star", to launch a missile straight into the heart of the enormous structure? Skywalker penetrates a long valley where the walls quickly move laterally, above and below the speeding spaceship; a very dramatic special effect, a special effect that was first "invented" at the end of the 1960s by a mathematician at Brown University, in Providence, Rhode Island, to study a topological surface. A 'subjective', as they say in film, virtual voyage within a topological geometric structure in order to better understand its properties. Something completely new for that time, using a technique that now seems obsolete, I would even say primitive.

The fact is those who work with special computer graphics effects have had to learn and comprehend the new possibilities mathematicians have constantly discovered as computer tools were further perfected and experiences, true experiments in mathematics and geometry, became more and more sophisticated.

The story that ends with *Star Wars* began many centuries, even millennia ago. When humanity had no idea of space, did not even consider the problem. It began with learning to count humanity and would take thousands of years to develop a precise and reliable enough method; to be able to measure, first a section of the earth's surface, then the surface of the earth, then the distance of the heavenly bodies and predict their movements; to be aware of the cyclical nature of astronomic events, predict the seasons. First numbers arrived in human culture; then figures, then forms and then mathematics was born, the science of quality and quantity.

The precise definition of mathematics should be clarified first. This question is not easily resolvable, in fact not even close. Furthermore, mathematicians seldom worry about it. They only need to know when they "do" mathematics. To those not interested in mathematics, who do not understand mathematics, the question seems completely superfluous.

But it is not for our story.

Star Wars, *The Death Star.*

What is Mathematics?

The famous French mathematician Jean Dieudonné in his vast study entitled *Pour l'honneur de l'esprit humain*, wrote that "the situation of mathematics within the framework of human activity is paradoxical". The fact is almost everyone recognizes mathematics as a fundamental discipline and necessary practically in every sector of science and technology. Furthermore, the opinion is fairly widespread that the mere fact of having a moderate understanding of mathematics opens the way to a growing number of work activities.

On the other hand, with the great distribution of calculators today, popular opinion is that the work of mathematicians has been in some sense surpassed if not made completely useless. Considering everyone had their first contact with mathematics through more or less banal calculations, Dieudonné observes once again that "the most widespread idea is that a mathematician is someone particularly well versed in calculations. Today, with the coming of calculators and their languages, the trend is to believe the mathematician is an individual very skilled in programming them and one who dedicates all their time to this activity."

If mathematics and what mathematicians do were really like this then architects should rightly ignore it.

It is tempting to conclude that any attempt to communicate what mathematics is today, what mathematicians do today, is useless anyway because, as André Weil writes: "Mathematics has the peculiarity that it cannot be understood by non-mathematicians". Or at times an idea of mathematics is given. This is what engineers have who, always in search of optimum values for their greatness, "see," as Dieudonné observes, "in mathematicians repositories for a treasure of formulas to furnish them on request". But if we are to understand, as the author of *The Man without Qualities* (1930), Robert Musil, notes "that an engineer concentrates completely on his specialty, instead of moving through the vast, free world of thought" then this is not true of mathematicians who "have a new logic and spirit in their essence".

If the new logic and spirit in their essence are in mathematics, then it is easy to see how mathematicians feel it worthwhile to make themselves understood.

For the mathematician Hardy:

> The mathematician, like the painter and poet, is a creator of forms. If the forms he creates are more durable than theirs, it is because his are made of ideas. The painter creates forms with symbols and colors, the poet with words. A painting can embody an "idea", but these are usually banal with no importance. In poetry, ideas count much more but their importance is usually exaggerated. […] The mathematician, on the other hand, has no other material to work with except ideas; therefore, the forms he creates have some chance of lasting longer since ideas wear out less than words.

Words so explicit they help understand why Robert Musil called the interest of the mathematician for his discipline *passion*. Mathematics, that uses only *ideas* to obtain its results, cannot only be more durable than poetry and painting, but aspires to be compared to these also in terms of purely esthetic evaluations. *Beauty* is for Hardy, and many mathematicians, one of the characteristics of mathematics.

Kline wrote in his book, *Mathematical Thought from Ancient to Modern Times*:

> Mathematics has determined the direction and content of a good part of philosophical thought, destroyed and reconstructed religious doctrines, constituted the crux of economic and political theories, molded the principal styles in painting, music, architecture and literature, procreated our logic and furnished the best answers we have to the fundamental questions on the nature of man and the universe. […] Finally, being an incomparably refined human creation, it offers satisfaction and esthetic values at least equal to those offered by any other sector in our culture.

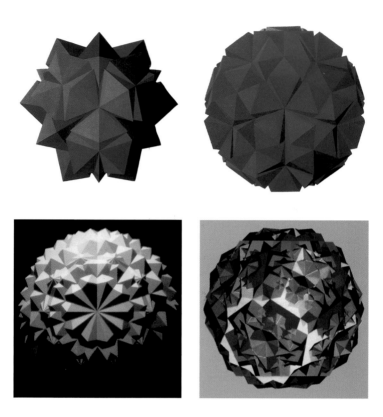

L. Saffaro. Top left: Il Poliedro M2, *oil, 1985; right:* I 360 triangoli, *oil, 1986. Bottom: software for the combination of platonic homo-centred polyhedrons, ENEA, Bologna, eng. Frattini and Cavazzini.*

An answer is still missing to the question of what is mathematics. For its non-philosophical character, the definition I love the best is by Richard Courant and Herbert Robbins in the introduction to their book, *What is Mathematics: An Elementary Approach to Idea and Methods*:

Over the centuries, mathematicians have considered the objects of their study, such as for example, numbers, points, etc., as things existing in themselves. Since these bodies have always challenged any attempt at adequate description, the idea slowly arose among 20th century mathematicians that the meaning of these objects as substantial things, even if it makes sense, has no sense in the field of mathematics. The only important affirmations regarding them do not refer to substantial reality, and establish only the relationships between «non-defined mathematical objects" and the rules that govern operations with these.

In the field of mathematical science, one cannot and must not discuss what points, lines and numbers effectively are. What is important and what corresponds to "verifiable" facts are structure and relationships, that two points determine a straight line, that numbers combine according to certain laws to form other numbers, etc. […] Fortunately, the creative mind forgets dogmatic philosophical opinions when they would block constructive discoveries. For scholars, just as for laymen, it is not philosophy but active experience alone that can answer the question: What is mathematics?

A definition that refuses to be a definition but that is still the best definition possible! With the words "structure" and "relationships" that should interest architects. What has been said up till now can be summarized with a phrase, again from Courant and Robbins: "As an expression of the human mind, mathematics reflects the active will, contemplative reason and desire for esthetic perfection. Its fundamental elements are logic and intuition, analysis and construction, generality and individuality."

Structure and relationships between objects for which nature is ignored. Greek mathematicians attempted to establish the object of mathematics, of geometry, thus 'inventing' not only the science of space, but space itself; the idea of space that has for hundreds of years remained the only one valid; Euclidean space, metric Euclidean space and the science of proportions.

The Creation of Mathematics

Morris Kline in his monumental *Mathematical Thought from Ancient to Modern Times* writes that, "in the history of civilization, the Greeks occupy a preeminent place; in the history of mathematics, they are the supreme event". If, in Kline's opinion, the first recognition that mathematics deals with abstractions can with some certainty be attributed to the Pythagoreans, then the best part of the work of Greek mathematicians is contained in the writings of Euclid and Apollonius. Euclid lived in Alexandria around 300 BC. His most famous work is *The Elements*. Though this work contained material from previous mathematicians, Euclid is definitely responsible for, as Kline again writes, "the particular choice of axioms, the arrangement of the theorems and several demonstrations, just as the cleanness and rigor of the demonstrations".

The Elements contain thirteen books. Book I contains the definitions and concepts used in the work.

Here are some of the definitions:

Definition 1. A point is what has no parts.

Definition 2. A line (curve) is length without width.

Definition 3. The ends of a line segment are points.

Definition 4. A straight line is one that lies equally with respect to its points.

Definition 5. A plane has only length and width.

Definition 6. The ends of a plane segment are lines.

Definition 7. A plane is what lies equally with respect to its straight lines.

Definition 23 is particularly interesting:

Straight lines are parallel when, being on the same plane and infinitely long in both directions, they do not meet in either of these directions.

Euclid then listed five postulates that were so clearly true they would be accepted for hundreds of years as indisputable.

Postulate 1. A straight line segment can be drawn joining any two points.

In particular the famous

Postulate 5 (on parallels). If two lines are drawn which intersect a third in such a way that the sum of the inner angles on one side is less than two right angles, then the two lines must inevitably intersect each other on that side if extended far enough.

In other words, given a straight line segment and a point outside it, only one single parallel line exists to this given straight line.

Mathematician Robert Osserman wrote in his beautiful book, *Poetry of the Universe*:

> Euclid's *Elements* made a deep impact on the psyche of the Western world. Originally viewed as both a tool and model for research in mathematics and other sciences, *The Elements* gradually evolved into a basic component of a standard education – a piece of intellectual equipment that every young student was expected to wrestle with and internalize. The appeal of *The Elements* has at least four distinct components. First, there is the sense of certainty – that in a world full of irrational beliefs and shaky speculations, the statements found in *The Elements* were proven true beyond a shadow of a doubt. And although certain features in both the assumptions and methods of reasoning used by Euclid have been questioned over the centuries, the astonishing fact is that after two thousand years, no one has ever found an actual "mistake" in *The Elements* – that is to say a statement that did not follow logically from the assumptions.

The importance of this statement should be emphasized. Not one "error" has been found in *The Elements* after two thousand years of study. Could mathematics be the main way to eternity? Osserman again states the second reason for the appeal of the Elements consists in the "power of the method. Starting from a very few explicitly laid-out assumptions, Euclid produced a dazzling series of consequences. This is the display of ingenuity employed in his proofs – not so different from the sort of ingenuity that adds to the appeal of a well-crafted detective story."

We could add a good novel, a good film, a good painting, or interesting architecture; in other words, the appeal of artistic creation. The final element Osserman underlines is precisely this esthetic aspect: "Finally, the objects of reasoning in the first books of *The Elements* are geometric shapes that have an aesthetic appeal all their own, quite apart from any formal reasoning that may be applied to them."

Kline adds:

> It seems clear that all the Greek philosophers who forged and shaped the Greek intellectual world valued the study of nature for the comprehension and appreciation of the reality resting upon it. Beginning with Pythagoras, practically every one of them asserted that nature was

mathematically designed. During the classical period, the doctrine of the mathematical design of nature was consolidated and research into its mathematical laws was institutionalized. Even if this doctrine did not motivate all mathematics created subsequently, once consolidated it was accepted and consciously pursued by most mathematicians for the entire period this doctrine maintained its influence, in other words until the second half of the 19th century. Even though a few Greeks, such as Ptolemy, realized mathematical theories were only human attempts to supply a coherent description, the belief that mathematical laws made up the truth around nature attracted some of the deepest, most noble thinkers to mathematics.

Words that are a true justification help me leap across thousands of years to reach the period when the grand design of Greek mathematics becomes not surpassed, no one could ever put into dispute their theorems and results, but instead profoundly changed. With a brief mention of the Renaissance when the texts of Greek mathematicians were rediscovered, translated and published, first among them *The Elements* of Euclid, and the intermingling of mathematicians, artists and architects would be one of the main pillars of the culture of the new Renaissance man.

For centuries, Euclidean geometry, the objects it defined, its postulates, axioms and theorems, were the "truth" in the world of nature. And as Plato said of the five regular solids of space, "I will concede to no one that there are bodies in the universe more beautiful than these". The solids Plato spoke of, described in his *Timaeus*, are the so-called *platonic solids*: the tetrahedron, octahedron, icosahedron, cube and dodecahedron. For thousands of years we have lived in the space imagined and described by Euclid. Architecture for centuries has followed the rules dictated by Greek culture: Euclidean geometry and the science of proportions.

A world constructed with images from the mathematical design of the universe, in an attempt to give deep meaning to the life of man. Man, his proportions, the matrix of the universe.

One of the celebrated quotes on mathematics comes from physicist Eugene Wigner: "The irrational efficiency of mathematics in the science of nature". Irrational given that the foundation of mathematics is an abstraction and therefore mathematics could appear even further from physical reality. Osserman again writes that, "this abstraction functions in various ways. First and foremost

Preclarissimus liber elementorum Euclidis perspicacissimi:in artem Geometrie incipit quã fœlicissime.

Punctus est cui pars nõ est. ¶ Linea est lõgitudo sine latitudine cui° quidẽ extremitates sũt duo pũcta. ¶ Linea recta ē ab uno pũcto ad aliũ breuissima extẽsio i extremitates suas utrũqʒ eoꝝ recipiẽs. ¶ Supficies ē que lõgitudinẽ & latitudinẽ tantũ hj:cuius termini quidẽ sũt linee. ¶ Supficies plana ē ab una linea ad aliã extẽsio i extremitates suas recipiens

De principiis p̄ se notis:& prio de diffinitionibus earundem.

¶ Angulus planus ē duarũ linearũ alternus cõtactus:quarum expãsio ē sup supficiẽ applicatioqʒ nõ directa. ¶ Quãdo aũt angulum continẽt due linee recte rectilineus angulus noiaſ. ¶ Quãdo recta linea sup rectã steterit duoqʒ angulí utrobiqʒ fuerit eqles:eoꝝ uterqʒ rect°erit. ¶ Lineaqʒ linee supstãs ei supstat ppendicularis uocaſ. ¶ Angulus uero qui recto maior ē obtus˜ sus dicit. ¶ Angulus uero minor recto acut° appellaſ. ¶ Termin°ē qd˜ uniuscuiusqʒ finis est. ¶ Figura ē q termiuo uel termis cõtinet. ¶ Circul°est figura plana ura qdẽ linea cõtẽta:q circũferẽtia noiaſ:ī cui° medio pũct° est:a quo oẽs linee recte ad circũferẽtiã exeũtes sibiiuicẽ sũt equales. Et hic qdẽ pũct˜ centrũ circuli dicit. ¶ Diameter circuli ē linea recta que sup eiˉ cenꜩ trãsiẽs extremitatesqʒ suas circũferẽtie applicans circulũ i duo media diuidit. ¶ Semicirculus ē figura plana diametro circuli & medietate circũferẽtie cõtẽta. ¶ Portio circuli ē figura plana recta linea & parte circũferẽtie cõtẽta:semicirculo quidẽ aut maior aut minor. ¶ Rectilinee figure sũt q rectis lineis cõtinenſ quaꝝ quedã trilatere que trib˜ rectis lineis:quedã quadrilatere que q̃tuor rectis lineis.quedã multilatere que pluribus q̃ quatuor rectis lineis cõtinenſ. ¶ Figuraꝝ trilateraꝝ:alia ē triãgul˜ hñs tria latera equalia. Alia triãgulus duo habens eqlia latera. Alia triãgulus triũ inequaliũ laterũ. Harum itẽq alia est orthogoniũ:unũ.ſ.rectũ angulũ habẽs. Alia ē ambligonium aliqdẽ obtusũ angulũ habens.Alia ē oxigonium:i qua tres anguli sũt acuti. ¶ Figuraꝝ aũt qdrilateraꝝ Alia ē qdratum quod ē eqlaterũ atqʒ rectangulũ.Alia ē tetragon°long°:que ē figura rectãgula:sed eqlatera nõ est. Alia ēst helmuaym:que ē equilatera:sed rectãgula non est.

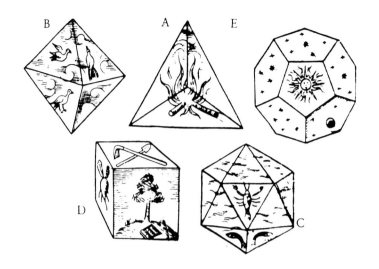

The five platonic solids, in J. Keplero, Harmonices Mundi Libri V, *Book V,* De Harmonia Perfectissima Motuum Cœlestium, *Linz 1619, p. 292.*

it possesses the power of universality that allows the application of a single rule in very different circumstances". One example should suffice. The algebra of logic was at the basis of development before calculating machines and modern computers. Alan Turing conceived the first idea of the modern computer somewhere around 1940. The logic at the basis of the modern computer guarantees the same machine can be adapted to practically any problem, from medicine to architecture, from the simulation of airplane wings to astrophysical research.

A second advantage is that it frequently brings clarity to what could be a confused situation. For example, the notions of "point" and "line" in Euclid are very clearly expressed and subject to much more simple rules than the points and straight lines of real life of which they are in fact an abstraction. Osserman underlines that "the danger lies in the fact that conclusions reached by applying the most simple rules to our abstractions may not be valid if then applied to objects originating in the physical world. Wegner's phrase brings to light the fact that these conclusions often function perfectly".

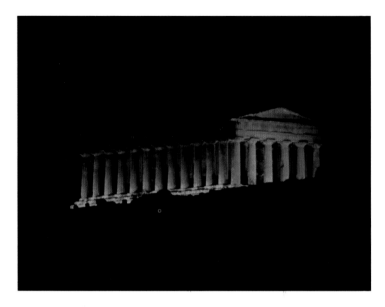

Athens, the Parthenon.

"The third great advantage of abstraction is that it allows our imagination great liberty, permitting us to devise new and alternative versions of reality; versions that may or may not correspond to something in the real world."

These motives doubtlessly made Euclidean geometry and *The Elements* one of the foundations of our way of conceiving the world and manner of living in it. Therefore it makes sense it took hundreds of years for this "beautiful abstract construction" to be in any way abandoned.

But doubt was found precisely where no one thought it could be. If those were the definitions, the objects of *The Elements*, and "evidently" from objective reality, then the postulates accepted as absolute truth could perhaps be demonstrated and therefore Euclid's constructions simplified to become in some sense more "elegant", more perfect.

The search for simplicity as a synonym for beauty has always been one of the greatest driving forces for mathematicians.

The fifth postulate on parallels should have been able to be

Raffaello Sanzio, La Scuola di Atene, *Vatican.*

demonstrated beginning with other assumptions. Mathematicians began to attempt to show how to obtain this type of result. And as happens many times in mathematics and science, the results obtained were completely different from those expected.

One of the ways demonstrations are formulated in mathematics is via the so-called method of demonstration by the absurd. If we want to demonstrate a certain phrase is true, we assume the opposite is true and if we arrive at any obvious contradiction, since there is no third way, the original phrase must be true.

If we want to show via the "absurd method" that the fifth postulate on parallels is true based on the others, we would suppose it is not true. The intent is obviously to arrive at clear contradictions that would assure the fifth postulate is true and derivable from others. In doing this, thus negating the validity of the fifth postulate, we arrive at inventing a new type of geometry, in fact many new types of geometry. The role of the only queen of space was taken from Euclidean geometry. In fact the idea itself of space would be modified, just as the idea of the universe in which we live. As Osserman proposed, we can represent three thousand years of geometric invention with the shape of a tree, the "geometree" with roots that stretch into a far away past and branches that represent the results of centuries of discoveries and creation.

When did the great upheaval occur and humanity discover it could no longer live in the reassuring Euclidean world as it had previously thought? Was the entire Euclidean vision of the world then abandoned?

Here begins the tale of an important character, the Square of *Flatland*, a character cited frequently even in books of architecture. Here is how Alicia Imperiale speaks of him citing Edward R. Tufte in *Envisioning Information*:

> Tufte examines a wide number of examples of designs and blueprints, static images that nevertheless constitute a rich deposit of space-time complexity. Even though we navigate daily through a three-dimensional space with our bodies and are capable of imagining greater dimensional organizations via mathematical calculations, Tufte maintains we are continuously forced to represent information on the infinite Flatland of paper and video screens. Avoiding this flat world, states Tufte, must be the fundamental objective of the visualization of information since all the fascinating worlds we seek to penetrate (physical, biological, imaginary, human) are inevitably and happily multidimensional in nature. Not like Flatland.

After this statement, the moment has come to enter *Flatland* and see if it is precisely as Tufte writes or if instead *Flatland* is not a land of the discovery and vision of worlds with many dimensions.

Space should have three dimensions [...] but why precisely three and not a fourth perpendicular to the other three. [...] I will not hide the fact from you that I have for some time occupied myself with four dimensional geometry."

H.G. Wells, *The Time Machine*, 1895

2. The New Freedom: The Infinite Space

I (the Square). "What therefore more easy than now to take his servant on a second journey into the blessed region of the Fourth Dimension, where I shall look down with him once more upon this land of Three Dimensions, and see the inside of every three-dimensioned house, the secrets of the solid earth, the treasures of the mines of Spaceland, and the intestines of every solid living creature, even the noble and adorable Spheres."

SPHERE. "But where is this land of Four Dimensions?"

I. "I know not: but doubtless my Teacher knows."

SPHERE. "Not I. There is no such land. The very idea of it is utterly inconceivable."

I. "Not inconceivable, my Lord, to me, and therefore still less inconceivable to my Master. Nay, I despair not that, even here, in this region of Three Dimensions, your Lordship's art may make the Fourth Dimension visible to me; just as in the Land of Two Dimensions my Teacher's skill would fain have opened the eyes of his blind servant to the invisible presence of a Third Dimension, though I saw it not."

The characters in this dialogue are two regular geometric figures. The first, the protagonist of the story, the narrating 'I', is the Square, an inhabitant of Flatland; the second character, treated with great deference by the other, is the Divine Sphere from the Land of Three Dimensions. We find ourselves in *Flatland*, the land of two dimensions. The Square himself suggests a way of understanding his world:

Imagine a vast sheet of paper on which straight Lines, Triangles, Squares, Pentagons, Hexagons, and other figures... move freely about, on or in the surface, but without the power of rising above or sinking below it, very much like shadows -- only hard with luminous edges.

Naturally in Flatland it is impossible to have "anything of what you call a 'solid' kind." The inhabitants of Flatland can in no way imagine the existence of three-dimensional objects given that a

"O day and night, but this is wondrous strange"

FLATLAND

Ten Dim Fire Dimen Eight D

Nine

No Dimensions
POINTLAND

One Dimension
LINELAND

A ROMANCE
OF MANY DIMENSIONS

By A Square

(Edwin A. Abbott)

Two Dimensions
FLATLAND

Three Dimensions
SPACELAND

" And therefore as a stranger give it welcome."

BASIL BLACKWELL . OXFORD

three-dimensional unit of measure must be available to *measure* a three-dimensional object; from their point of view, they would say only *luminous lines* exist that represent themselves, in other words the inhabitants, houses, trees of Flatland. Suppose you carefully place a triangle on a plane, a table, and imagine looking at it with your eye at the edge of the table; you would see only a line, a segment, writes Abbott; in reality, if the triangle were actually in only two dimensions you would see nothing, but the author, who incidentally was a mathematics teacher, solves this problem by observing that the sides of the figures are luminous and therefore visible.

Conclusion: a square in Flatland can have no idea of a Sphere; merely supposing the existence of three-dimensional figures brings such turmoil to the tranquility of this land that anyone even having thoughts of this kind is immediately arrested. Not only can no inhabitant have an idea of a Sphere but if, as in our case, a Sphere were to descend from space to visit Flatland, no one would recognize it because the only thing visible to two-dimensional eyes would be a line representing the section between the plan where the inhabitants of Flatland live and the Sphere. Unless... a Square meets a Sphere that helps him *leave the plane and move up into Space-land*.

The Square would feel what we would feel if someone pulled us up into the space of four dimensions:

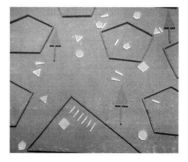

An unspeakable horror seized me. There was a darkness; then a dizzy, sickening sensation of sight that was not like seeing; I saw a Line that was no Line; Space that was not Space: I was myself, and not myself.... "Either this is madness or it is Hell." But anguish quickly gave way to

Three frames by the video Flatlandia *(1992), by Michele Emmer (© Michele Emmer, 2003).*

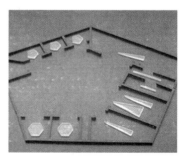

wonder: "A new world!" There stood before me, visibly incorporate, all that I had before inferred, conjectured, dreamed, of perfect Circular beauty. What seemed the centre of the Stranger's form lay open to my view: [...] a beautiful harmonious Something — for which I had no words; but you, my Readers in Spaceland, would call it the surface of the Sphere.

Alicia Imperiale speaks this way of the meeting:

In the science fiction classic [but are we really sure? My note], *Flatland*, a stranger, a Sphere turns to Mister Square. The Sphere explains to the Square the concept of height that is absolutely incomprehensible in the world of Flatland. He explains that he, the Sphere, a three-dimensional solid, on the two-dimensional plane of Flatland is perceived only as a circle, as a sequence of sections of the Sphere. The way the spatial and temporal information is recorded on the static plane of Flatland, on the screen of a computer or the space of a sheet of paper, is a question of utmost importance.

The word "time" has appeared. Is it correct to put time into play here? We shall see.

The meeting between the Divine Sphere and the Square is the central event in this very famous book, particularly in the English-speaking world, a book with the complete title *Flatland: A Romance of Many Dimensions*. The first edition was published anonymously in 1884. The author was an English theologian, Shakespearean scholar and mathematics teacher named Edwin Abbott Abbott (1838-1926). The first edition was issued without the author's name since Abbott was not convinced it was a good idea for him, a scholar of the Bible and Shakespeare, to have written this sort of book. How the Square comes to formulate the existence of the Fourth Dimension, after having discovered the Third, is a point worth mentioning. This will help understand how Abbott's book was written by an aficionado of mathematics who was aware of the questions debated by professional mathematicians of the time.

The Square, animated by true geometric spirit, got the idea from the discovery of the third dimension of attempting to go beyond it.

In Three Dimensions, did not a moving Square produce – did not this eye of mine behold it – that blessed Being, a Cube, with eight terminal points?

And in Four Dimensions shall not a moving Cube – alas, for Analogy, and alas for the Progress of Truth, if it be not so -- shall not, I say, the motion of a divine Cube result in a still more divine Organization with sixteen terminal points?

[...] And consequently does it not of necessity follow that the more divine offspring of the divine Cube in the Land of Four Dimensions, must have 8 bounding Cubes: and is not this also, as my Lord has taught me to believe, "strictly according to Analogy"?

[...] If I am wrong, I yield, and will no longer demand a Fourth Dimension; but, if I am right, my Lord will listen to reason. [...] And once there, shall we stay our upward course? In that blessed region of Four Dimensions, shall we linger at the threshold of the Fifth, and not enter therein? Ah, no!... Then, yielding to our intellectual onset, the gates of the Sixth Dimension shall fly open; after that a Seventh, and then an Eighth...

But the Sphere does not think this way. Though He had explained through analogy the passage from the second to the third dimension, he refuses to accept the same reasoning could be applied to arrive at higher dimensions. The Sphere finally denies his own reasoning: "Analogy! Nonsense: what analogy? [...] Whence this ill-timed impertinent request? And what mean you by saying that I am no longer the Perfection of all Beauty?" To then definitively conclude: "And in any case, however great may be the number of different explanations, no one has adopted or suggested the theory of a Fourth Dimension. Therefore, pray have done with this trifling, and let us return to business." The Square does not give up: "In vain did the Sphere, in his voice of thunder, reiterate his command of silence, and threaten me with the direst penalties if I persisted. Nothing could stem the flood of my ecstatic aspirations."

The mathematician rebels against dogmatic impositions. He wants to be able to utilize the instruments that have been made available to him. The Sphere knows only the third dimension. He wants no one to cast doubt on the fact that another more *beautiful* sphere does not exist in the Land of the Fourth Dimension. The revenge of the Sphere is not long in coming. The words of the Square are rudely interrupted by a great blow and the protagonist find himself catapulted into space further and further down where his return to the two-dimensional world of Flatland awaits him.

Abbott was perfectly aware that geometry had profoundly

changed over the course of the second half of the 19th century. He was aware Lobachevsky and Bolyai, between 1830 and 1850, had constructed the first examples of non-Euclidean geometry in which Euclid's famous fifth postulate on parallel lines was no longer valid.

Abbot's book falls within this environment. The author takes a position in favor of innovators and therefore the side of the protagonist, the Square, against the Sphere. At the time Abbot's book was published, mathematical literature had already seen the appearance of what could be called the *Geometry of the Fourth Dimension*, even if it is difficult to identify a precise date when a specific interest began in this aspect of geometry. We are obviously speaking exclusively of the fourth spatial dimension, in which the four coordinates of a point in space are all spatial. Arthur Eddington described the meeting between the Sphere and the Square in 1920 in the book *Space, Time and Gravitation*, a classic explanation of the theory of relativity, as the best explanatory piece on the fourth dimension. Eddington was considering four-dimensional space and asked himself to what extent the world imagined by Abbott agreed with the space-time of relativity. Eddington indicates three points in the story. The fact that when a four-dimensional body moves, its three-dimensional section may vary; this makes it possible for a rigid body to alter its form and dimensions. What is more, it is possible for a four-dimensional body to enter a completely closed three-dimensional room just as a three-dimensional being can place a pencil at any point inside a square without intersecting the sides. The Sphere behaves this way when he visits Flatland; the Square is naturally unable to *see* the visitor. Finally, it becomes possible to see the interior of a three-dimensional solid just as a three-dimensional being can see the interior of a square by observing it from a point external to the plane on which it lies. When a construction project is designed on a computer, we can see the interior without having to pass through the doors! The design is two-dimensional.

The Fourth Dimension

In Abbott's book, the four-dimensional cube or *hypercube* makes its first official appearance in literature; though rich in illus-

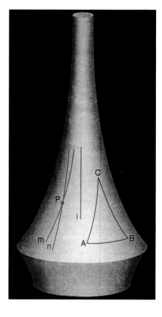

Left: consequences of the so-called elliptical non-Euclidean geometry of G.F.B. Riemann. On the convex surface of a sphere, straight lines m n 1, parallel to each other at the equator, converge and intersect at the poles while still remaining straight. The concept of parallelism does not exist in this space. In curvilinear triangle ABC, the sum of the interior angles is greater than 180°. Right: Consequences of the so-called hyperbolic non-Euclidean geometry of N.I. Lobachevsky-J. Bolyai. On the concave surface of the E. Beltrami pseudosphere, two straight lines m n passing through point P, converge while both are parallel to straight line 1. In curvilinear triangle ABC the sum of the internal angles is less than 180°.

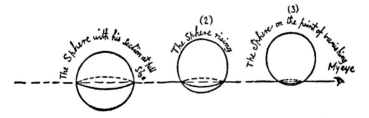

A drawing by Abbott in A. Eddington, Space, Time and Gravitation.

trations, the story does not include any designs of the Divine Cube. Mathematicians posed themselves the problem of visually representing the four-dimensional Divine Cube and other regular solids in four dimensions. How can we design a four-dimensional solid and therefore see a hypercube, since with our three-dimensional eyes, we can obviously never strictly see a four-dimensional object but only imagine it or use tricks such as those used by the Square?

One possible departure point is the analogy with the situation in three-dimensional space. The Sphere had stated that: "a Point has 0 sides; a Line, if I may so say, has 2 sides (for the points of a Line may be called by courtesy, its sides); a Square has 4 sides; 0, 2, 4; what Progression do you call that?" Square: "Arithmetical". Sphere. "And what is the next number?" Square: "Six". Sphere: "Exactly. […] The Cube which you will generate will be bounded by six sides, that is to say, six of your insides". So the Square, fascinated by this arithmetic progression, supported by the three-dimensional vision, goes further:

> And in Four Dimensions shall not a moving Cube – alas, for Analogy, and alas for the Progress of Truth, if it be not so – shall not, I say, the motion of a divine Cube result in a still more divine Organization with sixteen terminal points? Behold the infallible confirmation of the Series, 2, 4, 8, 16: is not this a Geometrical Progression? […] And consequently does it not of necessity follow that the more divine offspring of the divine Cube in the Land of Four Dimensions, must have 8 bounding Cubes: and is not this also, as my Lord has taught me to believe, "strictly according to Analogy"?

In this way, by translating a cube along a fourth axis perpendicular to the three-dimensional space in which the cube lies, we obtain a hypercube with 16 terminal points, 32 corners, 24 sides (that are square but appear distorted by perspective as quadrilaterals and rhombuses) and eight cells, where this term indicates a configuration of equal regular solids, in this case cubes, in such a way that each square face belongs to two cells and each corner to three cells.

In 1923, mathematician H.S.M. Coxeter began his work on geometry with more than three dimensions. The results of his work were published in the book *Regular Polytopes* in 1948, where he writes that to his knowledge only one or two people had ever had the ability to visualize hypersolids the same way mere mortals visualize solids. H.S.M. (Donald) Coxeter died on 31 March 2003 at more than ninety years old. His friends included, among others, Dutch graphic artist Maurits Cornelis Escher to whom he suggested Poincaré's models of non-Euclidean geometry for his engravings in the cycle *Circle Limit*. He spoke of his friendship with Escher in the film *The Fantastic World of Escher*.

A still more effective method, again based on analogy, was suggested by Poincaré in 1891:

> Just as it is possible to realize the perspective of a three-dimensional figure on a plane, so it is also possible to realize the perspective of a four-dimensional figure on a square of three (or two) dimensions. In geometry, doing this is no game. It is also possible to get, from one single figure, more perspectives from more different points of view. It is easy for us to represent these perspectives since they only have three dimensions. Let us imagine the different perspectives of one single object follow one from the other. […] So then nothing stops us from imagining such operations combine following the laws we would like; for example in such a way as to form a group that has the same structure as that of the movements of an invariable solid with four-dimensions. There is nothing in this that cannot be represented and nevertheless these sensations are exactly what an individual would experience endowed with a two-dimensional retina but who could move through four-dimensional space. In this sense, we can state it would possible to represent the fourth dimension.

Though defeated by force, the Square gets his revenge on the Sphere.

Ludwig Schläfli (1814-1895) was the first to study and determine the six regular solids in four-dimensional space. His work was not appreciated at the time and almost none of it was accepted for publication. In 1901, just six years after his death, his *Theorie der vielfachen Kontinuität* was published in which Schläfli dealt with *n*-dimensional geometry and in particular four-dimensional solids (that he called *Polyschem*). Excerpts of this work were published in English and French in 1855 and 1858 but went unobserved, probably because of the fact that, as Coxeter observed, their titles were too dry and tended to hide *the geometrical treasures they contained* or perhaps simply because those works were too advanced for their time. This is why many maintain that W. I. Stringham was the first to determine regular figures in four-dimensional space in his article "Regular Figures in n-dimensional Space" published almost thirty years after Schläfli's work. Stringham's work was an undeniable success.

Left: A model by J.H. Poincaré of hyperbolic non-Euclidean geometry applied here to a plane delimited by a circumference. The straight lines assume the aspect of arcs since an infinite number of lines parallel to a given line pass through one point. Right: M.C. Escher, Circle Limit III, *wood engraving in five colors, diameter 415 cm, 1959 (all M.C. Escher's works © 2003 Cordon Art B.W., Baarn, The Netherlands, all rights reserved).*

Art historian Linda D. Henderson, in her broad study *The Fourth Dimension and Non-Euclidean Geometry in Modern Art*, observes:

> The impact of Stringham's article was so remarkable that numerous references are found in the writings of both mathematicians and non-mathematicians at the beginning of the 20th century. Between 1900 and 1910, the different notions developed in the preceding century on the fourth dimension became more and more diffused, even outside the circle of scholars. This phenomenon was most widespread in the United States where a great number of popular magazines gave ample space to discussing this new concept. Interest reached its peak in 1909 when Scientific American sponsored a contest for *The Best Explanation of the Fourth Dimension* and received 245 contributions from all over the world. As Henderson underlines, all the participants interpreted the fourth dimension as a purely spatial phenomenon; time was never mentioned as the fourth dimension.

An important role in the popular diffusion of the fourth dimension was definitely Abbott's book, which quickly became a great success; a second edition was issued in 1884 and there have been nine reprints since 1915. Both mathematicians and writers have more than once quoted *Flatland*.

Mathematics, Cubism and Futurism

In *A Critique of Pure Reason*, Immanuel Kant characterized Euclidean Geometry as a priori knowledge, not based on experience, a part of our perception of the world, the essence itself of how we see the external world.

During the 19th century, the certainty that the geometry of the world was Euclidean would end. At the end of the 19th century, as underlined by art historian Linda D. Henderson, ideas that had been forming during the entire century among mathematicians (the surpassing of Euclidean geometry, spaces with more than three dimensions, the curvature of space) were spreading among intellectuals and artists through English, American and Russian science fiction. Space became relative.

The European artistic avant-garde could not help but be influenced by the new ideas in geometry. French mathematician E. Jouffret in his *Traité élémentaire de géométrie à quatre dimensions* begins with an analogy by quoting *Flatland*. Duchamp and several of the Cubists were aware of his book, which describes the different possible projections of four-dimensional objects in two and three-dimensional spaces.

Regarding probable knowledge of Jouffret's technique by some of the Cubists, Henderson observes that "in the portrait of Ambroise Vollard by Picasso from 1910 and in the Cavaliere perspective of Jouffret there is a remarkable resemblance in the use of triangular facets that represent a family of planes and angles considered from different points of view". Henderson's book is entirely dedicated to the influence mathematical theories had on the artistic avant-garde at the beginning of the 20th century, particularly Cubism and Futurism.

In the preface to one of the many reprints of the famous book *Du Cubisme* written by Albert Gleizes and Jean Metzinger in 1912, Daniel Robbins emphasizes that the work of the brothers Duchamp-Villon in the fields of mathematics, modern science and sociology was among the most important contributions to creating Cubism. The book by Gleizes and Metzinger was published in December 1912 just a few months after the art show called *Section d'Or* (The Golden Section), a name chosen because of the interest at the time in mathematics and proportions.

This quote from *Du Cubisme* is famous:

> Cubist painters studied the pictorial form and the space that surrounded it. This space was combined, carelessly, with both visual space as well as Euclidean space. Now Euclid and his postulates posed the undeformability of figures in movement.
>
> If we want to bring the space of painters closer to some sort of geometry, we should refer to scholars of non-Euclidean geometry, consider certain of Reiman's [cited with a single *n*] theorems.

Naturally, it is not important to establish how much the Cubists, or rather the authors of the manifesto *Du Cubisme*, might have understood of the new geometries including the Riemanian variety; what is important is that the idea that the geometry of space should no longer be considered exclusively Euclidean had by then also become absorbed into the cultured environment of the Parisian artistic avant-garde and others. In other words, thanks in part to the book by Abbott, it was an idea that circulated in the air. It was fashionable; it was modern. These words had to be used and attempts made to understand them even if the meaning was not fully understood. Henderson emphasizes that the fourth dimension never explicitly appears in *Du Cubisme* even if it mentions a "different type of space". While, for example, Guillaume Apollinaire in *Les peintres Cubistes* (1913) speaks of a new measure of space known as "the fourth dimension".

> Jusqu'à présent, les trois dimensions de la géométrie Euclidienne suffisaient aux inquiétudes que le sentiment de l'infini met dans l'âme des grands artistes. [...] Or, aujourd'hui, les savants ne s'en tiennent plus aux trois dimensions de la géométrie Euclidienne. Les peintres ont été amenés tout naturellement et, pour ainsi dire, par intuition, à se préoccuper de nouvelles mesures possibles de l'étendue que dans le langage des ateliers modernes on désignait toutes ensemble et briévement per le terme de "quatrième dimension".

It is a given fact artists in Paris at the beginning of the 20th century knew of Jouffret's book. Henderson reports an observation by Marcel Duchamp, who dedicated a vast part of his artistic activity to the fourth dimension: "The shadow caused by a four-dimensional figure is a three-dimensional shade in our space (see Jouffret, p. 186, last three lines)". Notes handwritten by Duchamp from 1912-1920 were published in a deluxe edition in 1966 titled

A l'infinitif. In them, he speaks explicitly about four-dimensional perspective.

Naturally, this does not mean in any way these were the only motivations and interests of Cubist artists, just consider the great importance of African masks. Again Apollinaire wrote that: "Les nouveaux peintres, pas plus que leurs anciens ne se sont proposé d'être des géomètres." This is no attempt to show how the artistic avant-garde used certain ideas or mathematical-geometric techniques, but rather an effort to understand how certain guiding ideas from science at the time profoundly influenced artists involved in avant-garde movements; mathematics as a source of suggestions and cultural stimuli especially regarding the idea of space.

For Henderson, the Parisian experience drove Boccioni to incorporating the fourth dimension "into Futurist art theory". In a letter to Barbantini in February 1912 he writes:

> This spiritualization will be a fact of pure mathematical values, of pure geometrical dimensions. […] If the objects are from mathematical values, the environment in which they live will be a particular rhythm of emotion that surrounds them. The graphic translation of this rhythm will be a state of form, a state of color. […] while at first sight this seems (for some) either philosophy or literature or mathematics, I feel it is pure painting!

In December 1913, Boccioni discussed in detail the role of the fourth dimension in Futurist art. In 1914, he included his observations in *Pittura scultura futuriste (Dinamismo plastico)*:

> Dynamism is the lyric conception of forms interpreted in the infinite manifestation of their relativity between absolute engine and relative engine, between environment and object, until forming the apparition of a whole: *environment + object*. […] Between the engine of rotation and engine of revolution; in other words it is life itself grasped in the form that life creates in its *infinite succession*. […] To this succession […] we add, through the intuitive search for the single form that gives continuity in space, … dynamic continuity as a single form. And it is not by chance that I say form and not line because dynamic form is a type of fourth dimension in painting and sculpture, that can not live perfectly without the complete affirmation of the three dimensions that determine its volume.

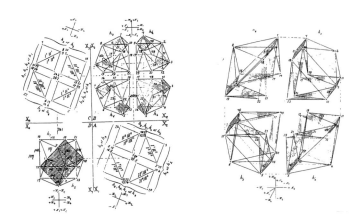

Two tables from Traité èlémentaire de gèometrie à quatre dimensions *by E. Jouffret (Paris 1903) that influenced Cubist painting.*

Left: Pablo Picasso, Woman with Guitar at the Piano, *1911, Prague, national Gallery. Right: Pablo Picasso,* Portrait of Ambroise Vollard, *1910, Moscow, Pus˘kin Museum.*

Umberto Boccioni, Forme uniche nella continuità dello spazio, *1913, Municipal Museum of Contemporary Art, Milan.*

Boccioni takes issue with the idea the Cubists had fully understood the concept of the fourth dimension:

> I remember having read that Cubism came close to the fourth dimension with its breaking up and unfolding the parts of the object on the flat surface of the painting. […] if it has ever been possible with artistic intuition to come close to the concept of the fourth dimension, then it is we Futurists who came close to it first. In fact, with the single form that gives continuity to space, we create a form that is the sum of the potential unfoldings of the three dimensions. Because of this, we do not give a measured and finite fourth dimension, but a continuous projection of the forces and forms intuited in their infinite unfolding.

The Cubist fourth dimension was static, abstract, that of the Futurists took into account the "form that was created from the succession of its states of motion". Boccioni was interested in the passage of a form of higher dimensions into our three-dimensional space, obtaining a continuous form in this passage, as in his famous 1913 sculpture *Forme uniche della continuità nello spazio* (*Unique Forms of Continuity in Space*); an idea very similar to the one that would lead, at the end of the 1960s, to obtaining the first continuous images of three-dimensional projections of four-dimensional objects with computer graphics.

The importance of mathematics and geometry in Futurism and Cubism should not be overestimated, however it remains an important element in understanding completely not only the way Cubists and Futurists thought but also the cultural role mathematics had in art and culture at the beginning of the 20th century, particularly regarding the idea of space.

The Hypercube

Given the complexity of designing projections with two or three dimensions, not all the hypersolids had the same good fortune in literature and art. The most "fortunate" has definitely been the hypercube, also called a *tesseract*.

Among the images published of the hypercube, those by H.P. Manning from 1914 became very well known even outside the circle of mathematicians. They represent two of the possible projections of a hypercube in three-dimensional space.

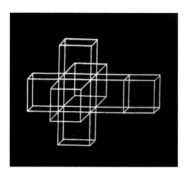
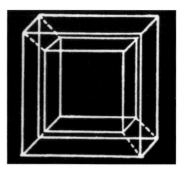

Images of a hypercube from Geometry of Four Dimensions, *by H.P. Manning (New York, 1914).*

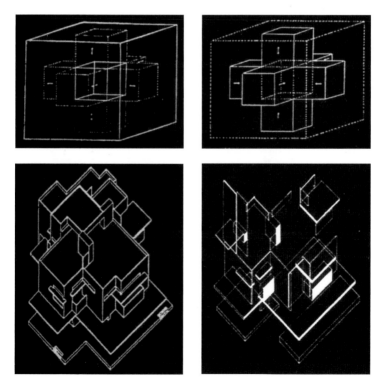

Theo van Doesburg and Cornelis Eesteren, design for a private house based on the idea of the hypercube (L'Architecture vivante, *1925).*

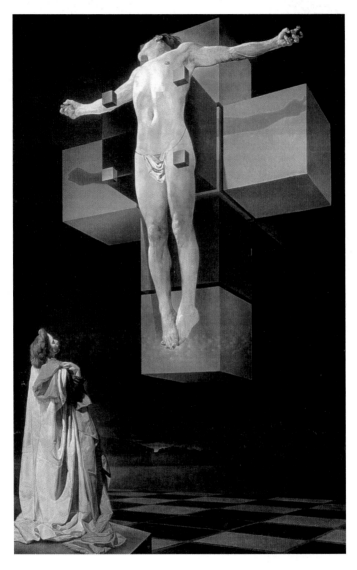

Construction of a hypercube based on the Manning model: Salvador Dalí, Crucifixion *(Corpus Hypercubus), 1954, New York, Metropolitan Museum. On the facing page: two series that show the first computer animation of a hypercube (from M. Noll, "A Computer Technique for Displaying n-Dimensional Hyperobjects",* in Association for Computer Machinery, ACM, *no. 10, 1967, p. 469).*

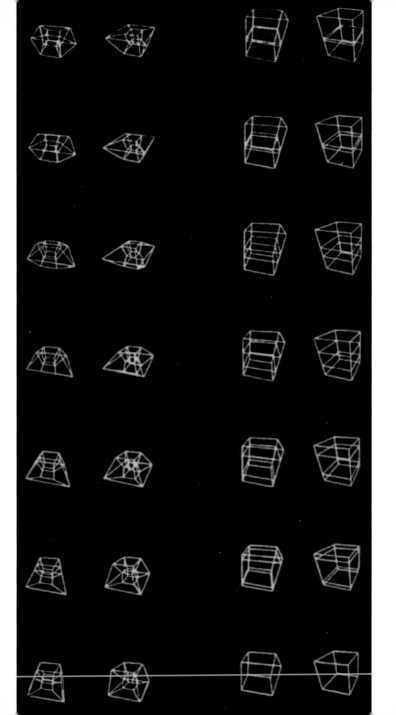

They would be used by many artists, including Theo van Doesburg and Salvador Dalì for his 1954 painting *Crucifixion* (*Corpus Hypercubus*). At the end of the 1960s, there was a revival in interest, among both mathematicians and artists, in four-dimensional objects; the reason was the appearance of computer graphics as a tool for helping satisfy the desire of the Square to see the Divine Sphere and the Divine Cube from four-dimensional space. An instrument was needed that allowed the exploration of that virtual world of the fourth dimension.

Possible projections of the hypercube in three-dimensional space (or rather perspective projections of the hypercube on a plane) began in 1967 with Michael Noll, one of the pioneers of computer graphics. In a work entitled *Displaying n-Dimensional Hyperobjects by Computers*, he wrote that any n-dimensional hyperobject could be manipulated mathematically via computer. This way it would possible to automatically design three-dimensional projections of a four-dimensional object rotating in space. Thus the strange distortions of three-dimensional projections obtained by rotating four-dimensional objects created the same problems for us as those of the inhabitants of Flatland. A reference to the tale by Abbott could not be avoided! Noll added that even if it were true that by utilizing the imagination it might be possible to extend to the fourth dimension the analogous knowledge of three-dimensional objects projected on a plane, nevertheless it would still remain impossible to visualize the four-dimensional object. His conclusions were pessimistic:

> In the beginning, it was thought a computer-generated film of a four-dimensional object might give us a more precise feeling of the visualization of the spatial fourth-dimension. […] Unfortunately, this is not the case and we are still in as much trouble as the inhabitants of Flatland.

So was it therefore impossible to realize the dream of the Square from Flatland? Noll had a plotter available at the time for designing different hypercube projections on paper.

Mathematician Thomas Banchoff took up Noll's idea. In 1978, he and his colleague at Brown University, Charles Strauss, created the first computer animated color film in which the hypercube could be seen moving in three-dimensional space. In 1977, Banchoff and his colleagues observed that, even if in theory all the ideas used for investigating three-dimensional space could be generalized to any higher dimension, nevertheless as regarded the four dimensions, it was still possible to broaden geometrical intuition quite a bit with a visual approach. The power of a computer graphics approach lies in the fact that it can construct any projection in three-dimensional space and manipulate it through rotations and projections as if it were a model placed in a room, observed via a video screen.

This type of approach in using the computer for mathematical research was new. It became possible to construct a surface on the video screen and move and transform it in such a way as to better understand its properties; a remarkable aid to intuition and research. The film *Hypercube* has become a classic of mathematical research. But more than that, the images of a hypercube rotating in space, turning itself inside out and back again like a glove, interested more than just mathematicians; the technique also interested the world of cinema; as already mentioned, several of Banchoff's assistants went to work at the Lucas Film computer center and contributed to special effects in the *Star Wars* series.

A brief sequence of the film *Hypercube*, that won the International Scientific Film Festival in 1979, was included in the hall dedicated to the Fourth Dimension at the Venice Biennale in 1986, testifying to the fact those never-before-seen images also had true aesthetic appeal. Coxeter writes that watching this rotating object always generates an attractive aura of mystery.

In 1987, Banchoff and his colleagues at Brown University realized another dream of the Square in Flatland: to see the four-dimensional Sphere, the hypersphere. Two mathematicians, H. Koçak and D. Laidlaw, explained the technique used to create the film *Hypersphere*:

> The great potential of computer graphics as a new tool for scientific investigation was recognized almost immediately by mathematicians. As instruments and software become more sophisticated, applications developed alongside them for various mathematical problems. […] The use of these new technologies showed itself to be very effective in the study of the geometry of surfaces in three and four-dimensional spaces. Efforts in this sector are very recent since obtaining realistic images of three or four-dimensional surfaces on a flat screen with only two dimensions requires costly instruments and very sophisticated software.

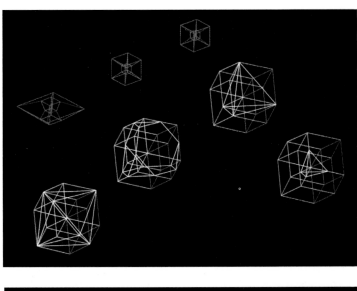

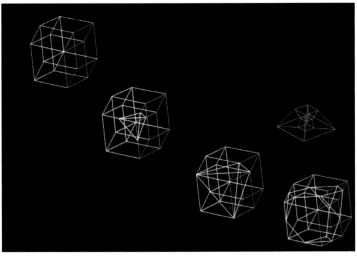

Hypercube in movement in a four-dimensional space: in the two images, a sequence from the film Hypercube: Projection and Slicing, *by T. Banchoff and C. Strauss, one of the first animations created with computer graphics.*

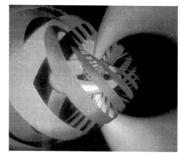

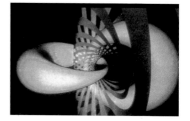

Images taken from the computer animated film Hypersphere, *by T. Banchoff, F. Bishop, H. Koçak and D. Margolis, Brown University, Providence, 1987.*

From the film Hypercube *(Eagle Pictures © 2003): Photographer and director Andrei Sekula, screenplay by Sean Hood and Ernie Barbarash, produced by Ernie Barbarash, set design Diana Magnus, visual effects Mr. X, Inc, Dennis Bernardi producer, Aaron Weintraub supervisor. Cast: Bruce Grey, Neil Crone, Geraint Wyn Davies, Kari Matchett, Matthew Ferguson, Grace Lynn Kung, Lindsay Connell, and Barbara Gordon.*

It took more than a hundred years but the Square's dream has finally come true. The Sphere has definitively lost his obscurantist battle! For this reason, a sequence of the film *Hypersphere* was inserted at the end of the film *Flatland* as homage to the Square's courage. It is now possible to see the hypercube move in three-dimensional space on a personal computer with very simple software. In summary, computer graphics has rendered it possible for everyone to reach that fantastic Land of the Fourth Dimension the Square could only imagine!

A film entitled *Hypercube* was released in 2003, the sequel to the film *Cube* from a few years before, directed by the Italo-Canadian director Vincenzo Natali. These titles obviously referred to, aside from the geometric object, the word "nightmare". Natali's film was a real nightmare in a cube. *Cube* narrated the story of seven people closed in a sort of enormous Rubik's Cube made up of many smaller cubes. By moving from one cube to the next, the protagonists seek to escape horrible death and find the exit. Among them is a mathematician who manages to break the code identifying the doors to the different cubes; a code based on multiples of prime numbers, a code developed by American mathematician, David Pravica.

If the Square from Flatland dreamed the Divine Cube with Four Dimensions, others conceived a sequel to the four dimensions of *Cube*; another director, Andrei Sekula, with screenwriters Sean Hood and Ernie Barbarash, the latter also producer.

The film *Hypercube* takes place in the 'Divine Cube' dreamed of by the Square. The story begins similar to the one in *Cube*; characters are gradually introduced who do not understand why they are imprisoned and attempt to escape. It is understood they must have been treated in some way (drugged?) and put inside the structure, actually a hypercube or *tesseract*.

Now how can a film progress inside a hypercube, i.e. inside a four-dimensional solid? This was the problem mathematicians Banchoff and Strauss faced in realizing their *Hypercube*.

These mathematical images were the source of inspiration for the environment of the new *Hypercube*. As mechanical, solid and tough as the environment was in *Cube*, the one in *Hypercube* is just as rarefied, all white, almost transparent. It makes us immediately think of being immersed in a virtual construction. This film contains many images created by mathematicians with a computer over the last few years. We see the solids, spoken of by Plato, up to the famous hypercube moving through space; proof of how certain mathematical ideas are transferred to the collective imagination a bit at a time; such as through a film! The hypercube materializes little by little in the film and becomes a perfect killing machine since all the corners of the figure are made of sharp cutting blades. It took more than a hundred years for the hypercube dreamed of by the Square in Flatland to become an object of mass consumption. But merely obtaining visually images of four-dimensional objects with each detail known from the mathematical point of view was not actually that interesting. Rather, it was the technique used, the possibility of exploring invisible, completely virtual worlds that helped computer graphics and computerized animation become a fantastic tool for investigating more than just mathematics. And what better than visualizing an object we cannot see in our three-dimensional world? The door was open for hypersurfaces in architecture as well.

Here is how one of the interpreters of hypersurface architecture, Marco Novak, perceives these ideas.

> Space, as we know, is both non-Euclidean and curved and multidimensional, containing more than three spatial dimensions. A space can be Euclidean and four dimensional, for example, or three dimensional and non-Euclidean. […] We now think of n-dimensional manifolds. Space and surfaces are thus intertwined: both are manifolds, the difference between hyperspace and hypersurface being that a hypersurface of a hyperspace of n-dimensions is a submanifold of $n-1$ dimensions. Thus the hypersurface of a hyperspace of four spatial dimensions is a space of three spatial dimensions, produced by an act of projection or section or screening.

For Imperiale, Novak, in proposing the concept of transarchitecture and hypersurfaces, implies the idea of 'trans-modern' understood as a conceptual bridge between the solid architecture of the modern era and the ephemeral architecture of the virtual. "He prefigures conceptual space in continuous development, created based on computer calculations in space, creating not a static concept, but rather an architecture of becoming." Though the computer screen appears two-dimensional, it has a spatial-temporal dimension that allows it to interact with hypersurfaces created

Marcos Novak, TransArchitectures: These types of architecture are created in the geometry of a multi-dimensional space and conceived as virtual environments in cyberspace; two images of the continuous degeneration of a paracube, utilizing a skeleton and a skin that can be deformed according to different variables and levels of fluidity.

mathematically in the space of the computer. "The hypersurface of the screen is the interface between real and virtual."

But what is the meaning of this word, 'hypersurfaces', as used in architecture? Stephen Perrella replies in his article "Hypersurface Theory: Architecture Culture".

In mathematics, a hypersurface is a surface in hyperspace, but in this context the mathematical term is existentialised. Hyperspace is four dimensional space, but here hypersurfaces are rethought to render a more complex notion of space-time information. This reprogramming is motivated by cultural forces that have the effect of superimposing existential sensibilities onto mathematical and material conditions, especially the recent topological explorations of architectural forms. While in mathematics, hypersurfaces exist in 'higher' or hyperdimensions, the abstractness of these mathematical dimensions is shifting, defecting or devolving into our lived cultural context.

Words, meanings, different potentialities, one single origin; the revolutionary mathematical idea that space exists only as a cultural category in which to define structures and rules.

3. The Enigma of Mathematics

The story is worth telling, at least in part, of how the idea of the computer was born since it is a very concrete example of an object human activity can no longer do without, an object born out of speculations that were also very abstract.

Observing me to look earnestly upon a Frame, which took up the greatest part of both the Length and Breadth of the Room, he said perhaps I might wonder to see him employed in a Project for improving speculative Knowledge by practical and mechanical Operations. But the World would soon be sensible of its Usefulness, and he flattered himself that a more noble exalted Thought never sprung in any other Man's Head. Every one knew how laborious the usual Method is of attaining to Arts and Sciences; whereas by his Contrivance, the most ignorant Person at a reasonable Charge, and with a little bodily Labour, may write Books in Philosophy, Poetry, Politicks, Law, Mathematicks and Theology, without the least Assistance from Genius or Study. He then led me to the Frame. […] The Superficies was composed of several bits of Wood, about the bigness of a Dye, but some larger than others. They were all linked together by slender Wires. These bits of Wood were covered on every Square with Paper pasted on them, and on these Papers were written all the Words of their Language, in their several Moods, Tenses, and Declensions, but without any Order. The Professor then desired me to observe, for he was going to set his Engine at Work. The Pupils at his Command took each of them hold of an Iron Handle, whereof there were forty fixed round the Edges of the Frame, and giving them a sudden turn, the whole Disposition of the Words was entirely changed. He then commanded six and thirty of the Lads to read the several Lines softly as they appeared upon the Frame; and where they found three or four Words together that might make part of a Sentence, they dictated to the four remaining Boys who were Scribes. This Work was repeated three or four Times, and at every turn the Engine was so contrived that the Words shifted into new Places, as the Square bits of Wood moved upside down. "

The narrator is Gulliver, describing the machine in question during his visit, in the course of his third voyages, to the great Academy of Lagado, capital of the kingdom of Balnibarbi, part of the Flying Island. Swift's book was published in 1726. If the imagi-

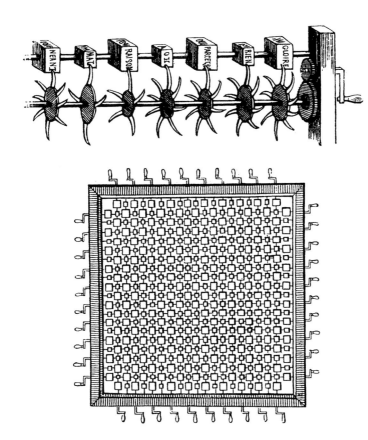

Drawings by J.J. Grandville for J. Swift's Gulliver's Travels.

nary machine described by Swift was a "linguistic" machine, the one imagined by the English mathematician Charles Babbage (1792-1871) was much more ambitious. In 1822, the first example was effectively built of a machine for differential calculus. "I thought," wrote Babbage, "that a machine capable of performing simple mathematical operations on its own would be of no great utility unless it was easy to make it carry out its work, as well as making it operate not only accurately but also rapidly." Even more ambitious was Babbage's project, on which he worked for thirty years, of an "analytical machine" that could be "taught" the mental process of "predicting". The machine would remain only a project and never be constructed. Morris Kline wrote: "At least until 1940, calculating machines were simply mechanical devices that only performed arithmetical calculations and had no influence on the course of mathematics". Andrew Hodges' book, *Alan Turing: The Enigma* is dedicated to one of the protagonists in the modern history of the computer. The title recalls both the enigma surrounding the death of the protagonist as well as his participation in decodifying the German code system called Enigma during the Second World War. We are speaking of Alan Turing (1912-1954). Little was known of Turing's life up till the 1970s. His activity during the War was considered top secret and his "scandalous" homosexuality caused him to be largely forgotten. "As a mathematician, Turing was far from committing the error of believing a concrete manifestation of thought would impoverish or devalue thought itself. What attracted him most in a mathematical formula was the fact it could have an effect on the physical world."

Turing had the idea of an "automatic machine" capable of reading a series of mathematical propositions and writing the verdict on their demonstrability. It was essential it do this without the interference of human judgment or intelligence.

The machine was meant to be capable of determining the following for each combination of configurations and symbols:

– write a new symbol in an empty box or leave the existing one unchanged or cancel it and leave the box empty;

– remain in the same configuration or change to another configuration;

– proceed to the box on the left or right or remain in the same position.

Writing by extension all this information intended to define an automatic machine, we have a "table of behavior" of finite dimensions. The table defines the machine in the sense that, independent of the physical existence of the machine, it contains all the information relevant to it. The table is the machine. Alan had transformed the vague concept of "defined method" or "mechanical process" into something very precise that was in fact the "table of behavior" Turing demonstrated that no "wonderful machine" existed capable of resolving all mathematical problems. But in doing so he discovered the idea of a universal machine capable of taking on the work of any machine. He showed how anything that can be done with a human calculator could also be done with a machine. So then one single machine reading the description of other machines on a tape might be capable of performing the equivalent of human activity; one single machine capable of taking the place of the human calculator! An electric brain! A Turing Machine. The war would give important impetus to this or better yet the activity of counter spying.

Enigma: Computers and Submarines

At the beginning of the Second World War, the British spy organization, known from time to time as either SIS or MI6, controlled the GCCS (Government Code and Cipher School) that had two assignments: "Study the methods of communication in code used by the foreign powers and express opinions on the security of British codes and ciphers." In 1937, the GCCS had a great problem; a machine called Enigma.

> It was at that point a proven fact that, as opposed to their Italian and Japanese counterparts, the German army, navy and probably air force as well, along with other state bodies and organizations such as the railroads and SS, used different versions of the same code system for all except their tactical communication: the Enigma machine. The machine was introduced in the 1920s but since then the Germans had made it more secure with subsequent modifications. In 1937, the GCCS managed to decode the key to a less perfected and therefore less secure model of the machine used by the Germans, Italians and the armed forces of Fascist Spain. But, apart from this, Enigma remained an unbreakable machine and it appeared probable it would continue to be so.

The central section of Hodges' book is dedicated to the role the English mathematician played in the British secret service. In 1939, Turing presented a request to the Royal Society for financing the construction of a machine that would be used for a specific mathematical problem: the calculation of zeros from the Zeta function. Though the bronze gears for the machine were built, the machine would never go into function. Given his experience on the "machine" and his interest for ciphers and codes, on 4 September

Alan Turing.

1939, Turing came to Bletchley Park where the headquarters of the GCCS had been established. Along with other mathematicians and physicists, he would contribute to decoding the German Enigma. Turing was already interested in what the most general form possible might be of a code or cipher. Furthermore, each form of code could be considered a complicated mechanical process that contained not only the rules of addition and substitution but also those designed to find, apply and communicate the methodology of cryptography. In other words, it entered into the scheme of the Turing machine; the irrational utility of mathematics.

The German Enigma used electric circuits to automatically perform a series of alphabetical substitutions. The machine had no fixed state; after putting the first letter of the message into code, a system of rotors turned to generate a new circuit of connections between entrance and exit. For a machine with 26 letters and three rotors, as the Enigma was at the beginning, there were 17,576 possible states. Furthermore, the rotors could be removed and remounted in different positions. Thus there were six possible positions and a total of 6 X 17,576 = 105,456 different substitutions. What is more, each rotor had a ring with the 26 letters of the alphabet that allowed further variations and finally there was a panel, a board of alphabetical commutations with electric jacks. This was the precise detail that distinguished the military Enigma from the others. At any moment a further exchange of letters could be performed. There were 1,305,093,289,500 different states for a three-rotor Enigma machine. Considering during the war the Germans built an Enigma with up to eight rotors, in addition to adding a control panel at the exit, it is easy to understand how they were convinced for the entire duration of the war no one could have ever decodified their system. The fundamental principal of the Enigma machine was that the rotors, rings and alphabetical communication panel were set in a certain way, after which automatically turning rotors encoded the message. For this to work in a practical communication system, the initial state of the machine had to also be known by the recipient.

The weak point of the system was that for one entire day all the operators of the network used exactly the same state of the machine for the first six letters of their messages. And the six letters were always the encryption of a triplet repeated twice. At the beginning of 1940, Turing proposed translating his idea into a project: contradiction and coherency as conditions under which the alphabetical framework of the Enigma could be surprised were concepts that had to do with a practical and decidedly finite problem, but the analogy was still impressive with the formalistic concept of mathematics in which mechanical operations follow from logical implications. The principal was surprisingly similar to mathematical logic, which attempts to get the maximum number possible of conclusions from a group of involved axioms. The new machine, called "Bomb" like all the others, was constructed in a very short time. On 22 May 1940, the GCCS was capable of deciphering the system used by the Luftwaffe. On 7 May 1941, an Enigma machine was captured with its instructions and for the first time information could be collected almost in real time, in other words useful for intervention. This permitted the destruction of ships sent to resupply the Bismarck in the Atlantic. This fact convinced the Germans the English knew something. However, they did not think, and would never think, their system had been identified. They thought there had been a spy working as a double agent. Naturally they changed the alphabetical setting, which meant the GCCS had to reset their equipment to zero and start over from the beginning. The advantage was they understood the system and therefore only had to discover the new key. By August 1941, the English were capable of deciphering any message in less than 36 hours. On 1 February 1942, German submarines changed their encoding system. The English "Bombs" were useless: they had to start over. There were thirty British "Bombs" when, with the entrance of the Americans in the war, the analogous but better financed secret service across the Atlantic began constructing its own "Bombs" in greater numbers than the English. Alan Turing was entrusted with the task of coordinating the two groups. At

Images from the film Enigma, *© Jagged Film, kind permission Istituto Luce, Rome.*

this point, the decodification system had become very refined. At the end of 1943, U-Boats were visible at a great distance; the English knew their positions more precisely than their own command.

Speed was naturally essential in being able to exploit the advantage of this decoding. This was one of the reasons electronic technology, in its early stages at the time, was introduced. In December 1943, the first completely electronic machine, Colossus, went into operation. Turing had already shifted from central operations (Bletchley Park had grown to an operation with 10,000 people) and was becoming more interested in problems connected to the question of storing the data the machine processed, what we call "memory". In 1945, a lot of water had passed under the bridge and the instruction book that had been something fantastic ten years earlier, just as the theoretical logic machines, had become something extremely concrete and practical.

Turing wrote in 1948:

> An infinity of different machines to perform different tasks is not necessary. Only one would be sufficient. Engineering problems that arise when you have to produce various machines for different tasks would be transformed into a task at the "work bench" in 'programming' the universal machine to carry out these tasks.

In 1945, Turing conceived the idea of the 'computer', in other words the automatic electronic digital calculator with an internal memory in the program. In 1954, Turing committed suicide by eating an apple soaked in poison. In 1953, he had been condemned to a yearlong hormone cure for homosexuality.

But the computer had entered the scene.

4. Topology

"Around the middle of the 19th century, geometry began to develop in a completely different way that was destined to quickly become one of the great forces in modern mathematics."

The words of Courant and Robbins in their famous book, *What is Mathematics?* "This new field, called *analysis situ* or topology, has as its object the study of the property of geometric figures that persist even when the figures undergo deformations so profound as to lose all their metric and projective characteristics."

As we told, the official birth of that sector of mathematics now called topology occurred with the book *Analysis Situs* ("topology" is the Greek version of the Latin name) published by French mathematician Henri Poincaré in 1895. Poincaré defined topology as the science that lets us know the qualitative properties of geometric figures not only in ordinary space but also in space with more than three dimensions. The object of topology is therefore the study of the properties of geometric figures that remain invariant even though they undergo such profound deformations they lose all their metric and projective properties such as form and dimensions. Geometric figures thus maintain their qualitative properties. Consider a figure constructed arbitrarily with deformable material on which neither cutting nor welding are possible; there are properties that are conserved when a figure so constructed is deformed at will.

In 1858, German mathematician and astronomer August Ferdinand Möbius (1790-1868) described for the first time, in a presentation at the Academy of Science in Paris, a new surface in three-dimensional space, a surface today known as the Möbius Strip. In his work, Möbius explained how to very simply construct the surface that today carries his name: take a rectangular strip of paper of sufficient length. If A, B, C, D indicate the vertices of the paper rectangle, proceed in this manner: holding with one hand one end of the strip (for example AB), on the other end, CD, perform a 180° turn along the horizontal axis of the strip in such a way as to bring together A with D and B with C. The construction of the Möbius Strip is complete! The surface has been deformed, with no cuts or tears, and the rotation carried out on a part of the strip has profoundly modified its properties. This new surface has interesting qualities. One lies in the fact that if you run a finger

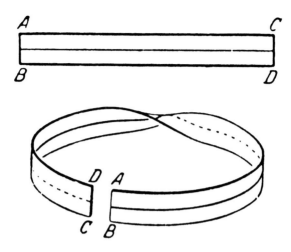

The Möbius Strip.

along the axis, you realize you can run the entire course and return exactly to the starting point without crossing edge of the strip; i.e. the Möbius Strip has only one side, not two like the external and internal ones for example in a cylindrical surface. Cylindrical surfaces are created with the ABCD strip by simply attaching the two sides, AB and CD, to each other. The entire surface of the Strip can be painted by proceeding along its horizontal axis without ever either taking the brush off the paper or crossing the edge of the surface. The same operation with a cylindrical surface would involve starting with the external face but also crossing one of the two edges that separate the external surface from the internal surface to paint the internal face, something unnecessary in the case of the Möbius Strip. With a cylindrical surface, you will never arrive at the lower edge by running a finger along the upper edge. In the case of the Möbius Strip, you can run along the entire edge from any point and return to the point of departure. In other words, it has only one edge. All this has important consequences from the topological point of view. Among other things, the Möbius Strip is the first example of a surface on which an orientation, i.e. a direction of movement, cannot be set.

Courant and Robbins again write:

A.F. Möbius, Zur Theorie der Plyeder und der Elementarverwandtschaft, *in* Gesammelte Werke, *vol. 2, Leipzig 1886, p. 515.*

First, the newness of the methods used in this new field gave no way to mathematicians to present their results in the traditional deductive form of elementary geometry. Instead, pioneers like Poincaré were forced to base themselves largely on geometric intuition. Even today [Courant and Robbins' book was from 1941] a scholar of topology would find that insisting too much on the formal rigors of exposition would lead to easily losing sight of the essential geometric content of a quantity of formal particulars.

The key term here is "geometric intuition". Obviously, mathematicians over the course of the years have attempted to bring topology into the realm of rigorous mathematics. But that aspect of intuition has remained. Precisely these two aspects, one of deformations that still conserve some properties of the geometric figure, and one of intuition, both play a fundamental role in the idea of space and form that began in the 19th century and have continued till today. First artists, then much later architects would *intuit* some ideas from topology over the course of the decades. The story is worth remembering of the discovery of a topological form by a great artist of the 20th century. A form that already existed in the world of mathematical ideas when the artist discovered it. But not just there; examples were found of the Möbius Strip, the surface we are speaking of, among decorations for the horses of the guard of the Tsar of Russia (17th century) and even in several Roman mosaics. So much so that ancient art scholar Lorraine L. Larison wrote that, "there is evident proof of a discovery of the Möbius Strip and appreciation of its particular properties by Roman mosaicists from the 3rd century".

This leads us to think the Möbius Strip might be a sort of archetypal form rediscovered over the course of the centuries.

The mathematical symbol for the infinite.

If the surface has an important place in topology because of its properties, then these same properties have greatly interested artists, painters, graphic artists and even poets. The ability to follow the entire surface, without ever detaching from the interior of the surface itself, was seen as a symbol of the *infinite*. Graphically, the mathematical symbol for the infinite, ∞, resembles a Möbius Strip seen in perspective. Le Corbusier also used this symbol in some Cubist paintings. But the discovery I want to communicate regards the great 20th-century artist and architect, Max Bill, who died in 1994. Here is what Bill wrote in the article "How I Started to Make Surfaces with One Side" when he discovered the Möbius surfaces. (Bill called his sculptures shaped like a Möbius Strip *Endless Ribbons*.)

Marcel Breuer, my old friend from the Bauhaus, was responsible for my one-sided sculptures. Here is how it happened. In 1935 in Zurich, along with Emile and Alfred Roth, I was constructing the Doldertal houses that had quite a following at that time. One day Marcel told me he had received the assignment to build a model house for an exhibit in London where everything, even the small fireplace, had to be electric. It was clear to us that an electric fireplace that shines but has no fire was not the most attractive object. Marcel asked me if I would like to make a sculpture to put over it. I began to search for a solution, a structure that could be hung over the fireplace and maybe spin in the ascending current of air and, thanks to its form and movement, would act as a substitute for the flames. Art instead of fire! After long experiments, I found a solution that seemed reasonable to me.

Max Bill, Endless Ribbon, *diorite, 150 x 100 x120 cm, 1935-1953.*

The interesting thing to note is that Bill thought he had found a completely new form. An even more curious fact, he discovered (invented?) this by playing with a strip of paper, the same way Möbius had discovered it years earlier!

> Little time had passed before someone congratulated me on my fresh and original reinterpretation of the Egyptian symbol of the infinite and the Moebius Strip. I had never heard mention of either one or the other. My mathematical knowledge had never gone beyond common architectural calculations and I had no great interest in mathematics.

The *Strip without End* was presented for the first time at the Milan Triennale in 1936. Bill wrote:

> As early as the 1940s I had thought about topological problems. I developed a sort of logic of forms from these. There were two reasons I continued to be attracted by this particular theme: 1) the idea of an infinite surface that is nevertheless finite, i.e. the idea of an infinite finite; 2) the possibility of developing surfaces that, because of intrinsic laws, lead

almost inevitably to a formation that proves the existence of esthetic reality. But both 1) as well as 2) also indicated another direction. If non-oriented topological structures existed only in virtue of their esthetic reality, then, despite their exactitude, I would never have been satisfied. I am convinced that the foundation of their effectiveness lies in part in their symbolic value. They are models for reflection and contemplation.

There is no doubt that Max Bill's fame and the presence of his *Endless Ribbons* in parks and museums worldwide has noticeably contributed to making the Möbius Strip famous even among we mathematicians. It could be said that, just as in the case of the fourth dimension, the hypercube has struck the imagination more than any other object. In the case of topology, this role went to the Möbius Strip along with another very special shape known as the "Klein Bottle". The Klein Bottle can be created beginning with a Möbius Strip carrying out the operations that conserve the property of having a single side. The Klein Bottle is also a one-sided surface that is closed but nevertheless has no interior or exterior. Glass models have been constructed of it.

These forms that interested Max Bill so much in the 1930s could not help but interest architects, even if several years would pass. It would take the diffusion of computer graphics that allow the visualization of those above-mentioned mathematical objects, in other words help support intuition that otherwise, for one who is not a mathematician, is difficult to manipulate.

Alicia Imperiale wrote in the chapter "Topological Surfaces":

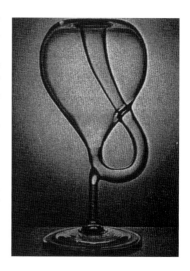

Klein bottle.

> Architects Ben van Berkel and Caroline Bos of UN Studio discuss the impact on architecture of new scientific discoveries [where "new" should be considered with a certain indulgence!]. Scientific discoveries have radically changed the definition of the term "Space",

72

Ben van Berkel (UN Studio/van Berkel & Bos), Möbius House, *Het Gooi, Amsterdam, 1993-97. The Möbius strip was used as a conceptual reference for developing this design; Möbius House is, as its name implies, organized around a continuous course that turns and folds back onto itself. The building is conceived in relation to distinct cycles of activity, with trajectories that interconnect according to a ring-*

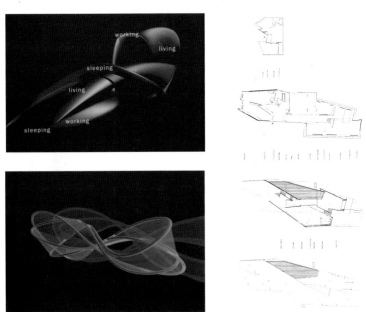

Diagrams.

Plans.

shaped diagram, so that different ways of living in the house are combined in a condition of sharing and, at the same time, separation of spaces intended for the family, individual and working lives of two people. The design is constructed in two folded bodies intertwined with one another in a figure eight and with continuous co-penetration of the internal and external faces of the volumes.

Diagram.

Möbius House, interior.

attributing a topological form to it. Instead of a static model of constituent elements, space is perceived as something malleable, changeable, and its organization, its division, its appropriation becomes elastic.

Here is the role of topology as seen by an architect:

Topology is the study of the behavior of a structure of surfaces that undergo deformation. The surface records the changes of the differential space-time shifts in a continuous deformation. This brings further potentialities for architectural deformation. The continuous deformation of a surface can lead to the intersection of external and internal planes in a continuous morphological change, just as in the Möbius Strip. Architects use this topological form in building design by inserting differential fields of space and time into an otherwise static structure.

Naturally several words and ideas are also deformed in passing from a strictly scientific to an artistic environment seen from a different point of view. But this is in fact neither a problem nor meant to be a criticism. These ideas circulate freely and everyone interprets them in their own way, attempting to grasp, as in topology, their essence. The role of computer graphics is essential in all this since they allow the insertion of that time deformation variable that would otherwise be unthinkable as well as unrealizable.

Imperiale continues regarding the Möbius Strip:

The Van Berkel house inspired by the Möbius Strip (Möbius House) is designed as a programmatically continuous structure that integrates the continuous change of sliding dialectic pairs that flow into each other, from interior to exterior, from work activities to leisure time, from supporting structure to non-supporting structure.

Obviously, at times intuition can lead to assumptions that are not completely correct: "Architects maintain that the Möbius model, the Klein Bottle, or other non-orientable geometric structures, are interesting because they are self-intersecting and have no interior closed space." The Klein Bottle has the property of never intersecting itself. It is a closed surface even though it has neither interior nor exterior. Nevertheless, these "imprecisions", we might say, of language do not impede "obtaining an integral structure, on which different active forces work, that acts like a natural landscape."

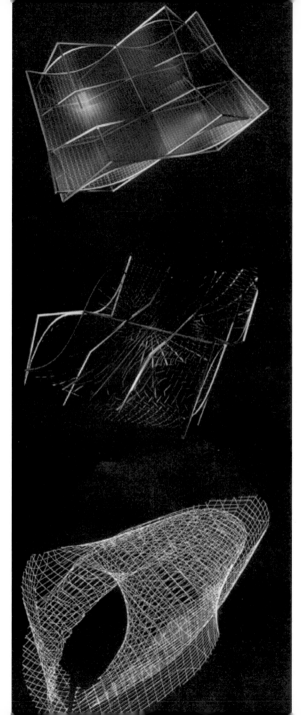

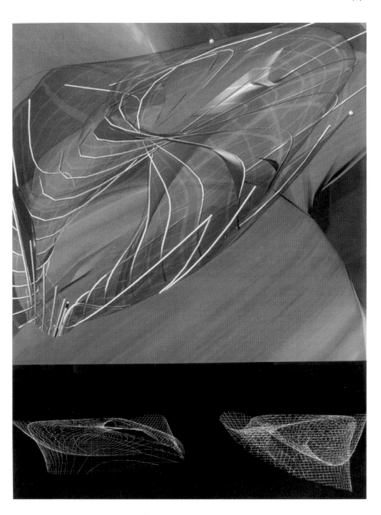

Stephen Perrella and Rebecca Carpenter, The Möbius House Study, *1997-98. This study was developed beginning with a membrane-diagram that was three-dimensionally manipulated through variations performed by animation software. These are topological manipulations of a surface, called improperly by the designers "hypersurfaces", tending toward a transverse architectural condition in which binary notions of internal and external are surpassed in favor of a spatial interconnection.*

In fact, the Klein Bottle, writes Van Berkel, "can be translated into a channeling system that incorporates all the elements it encounters and makes them precipitate into a new type of internally connected integral organization". Note the words "integral" and "internally connected" have a precise meaning in mathematics. But this is not a problem here because "the diagrams of these topological surfaces are not used in architecture in a rigorously mathematical manner but rather constitute abstract diagrams, three-dimensional models that allow architects to incorporate differentiated ideas of space and time into architecture."

Max Bill wrote something similar in 1949 regarding the links between art, form and mathematics: "By mathematical approach we must not mean what is generally called calculated art. Up till now all artistic manifestations have been founded, to a greater or lesser extent, on geometric structures and divisions." Even in modern art, artists have used regulating methods based on calculations since these elements, alongside more personal and emotional elements, gave *balance* and *harmony* to sculpted works. But according to Bill, these methods had however become more and more superficial, since, aside from the exception of the theory of perspective, the repertory of methods used by artists stopped at the Ancient Egyptian era. The new fact occurred at the beginning of the 20th century: "The starting point for a new concept could probably be attributed to Kandinsky who, in his 1912 book *Über das Geistige in der Kunst*, set the premises for an art which would substitute mathematical concepts for the imagination of the artist."

Mondrian, who distanced himself further than anyone else from the traditional concept of art, wrote:

Neoplasticism has its roots in Cubism. It could also be called abstract-real painting because the abstract can be expressed by a plastic reality in painting. This composition of colored rectangular planes expresses the deeper reality that comes through the plastic expression of relationships and not through natural appearance. [...] The new plastic poses its problems in esthetic balance and thus expresses the new harmony.

Bill believed Mondrian had exhausted the final possibilities that remained in painting.

I believe it is possible to develop an art based largely on a mathematical concept. [...] Mathematics is not only one of the essential means of primary thought, and therefore one of the recourses necessary for aware-ness of surrounding reality, but also in its fundamental elements, a science of proportions, of behavior from object to object, from group to group, from movement to movement. And since this science carries these funda-mental elements in itself and places them in significant relationships, it is natural that similar facts can be represented, transformed into images.

Furthermore, Bill adds, these mathematical representations, these limited cases in which mathematics is plastically represented, have an irrefutable esthetic effect. And here is the definition of what a mathematical concept of art must be:

> The mathematical concept of art is not mathematics in the strictest sense of the term, and we could also say it would be difficult for this method to use what is understood as exact mathematics. It is rather a configuration of rhythms and relationships, of laws that have their indi-vidual origin in the same way mathematics has its original innovative ele-ments in the thought of its innovators.

To be convincing, Bill needs to supply examples, examples inter-esting from his point of view as an artist, in other words examples of those that call the mysteries of mathematical problems "the 'indescribable' of space, the distancing and nearing of the infinite, the surprise of a space that begins in one place and ends in anoth-er, that is simultaneously the same, limiting with no exact limits, parallel lines that intersect and infinity that returns to itself." The Möbius Strip, obviously.

As has been said, even if a bit late, architects finally became aware of the new scientific discoveries in the field of topology. And aside from beginning to design and build, they also began to think and reflect. In her 1999 doctoral thesis, Architecture and Topology: *For a Spatial Theory of Architecture*, Giuseppa Di Cristina writes:

> The final conquest of architecture is space. This is generated through a sort of positional logic of the elements, i.e. through an arrangement that generates spatial relations; the formal value is thus substituted by the spa-tial value of the configuration. What is important is not so much the aspect of the exterior form as its spatial quality and therefore topological geometry of non-rigid figures with no "measurements". This is not some-thing purely abstract that comes before architecture, but rather the tracks left by that modality of action in the spatial concretization of architecture.

Piet Mondrian, Composition in Red, Yellow and Blue, *1937-1942.*

In her preface, "The Topological Tendency in Architecture", to a book published in 2001 on *Architecture and Science*, Di Cristina clarifies:

> The articles here bear witness to the interweaving of this architectural neo-avant-garde with scientific mathematical thought, in particular topological thought: although no proper theory of topological architecture has been yet formulated, one could nevertheless speak of a topological tendency in architects at both theoretical and operative levels. [...] In particular developments in modern geometry or mathematics,

V. Kandinskij, Black and Violet, *oil on canvas, 1923.*

perceptual psychology and computer graphics have influenced the present renewal of architecture and the evolution of architectural thought. What most interests architects who theorize about the logic of curvilinearity and pliancy is the meaning of "event", "evolution", and "process", that is, of the dynamism that is innate in the fluid and flexible configurations of what is now called "topological architecture". Architectural topology means the dynamic variation of form facilitated by computer-based technologies, computer-assisted design and animation software. The topologising of architectural form according to dynamic and complex configurations leads architectural design to a renewed and often spectacular plasticity, in the wake of the Baroque and of organic Expressionism.

Here is what Stephen Perrella means by "architectural topology":

Architectural topology is the mutation of form, structure, context and programme into interwoven patterns and complex dynamics. Over the past several years, a design sensibility has unfolded whereby architectural surfaces and the topologising of form are systematically explored and infolded into various architectural programmes. Influenced by the inherent

82

Peter Eisenman, Church for the Year 2000, Rome, 1996. The explicit conceptual reference made during the figurative design process was to the transitory condition of a liquid crystal, i.e. a state of suspension between the static condition of the crystal and the fluid state of liquid. The forms of the church were developed using diagrams of deformation that simulate distortions in the different phases of the molecular states of crystals. Simultaneously, the process of conformation of the project was controlled by building studio models with images that suggested an idea of polyhedric space constructed through the reticulation of masses folded according to simple decompositions of faceted surfaces, which, evolving according to a growing and extending character, make the church an object halfway between the idea of the finite and the infinite.

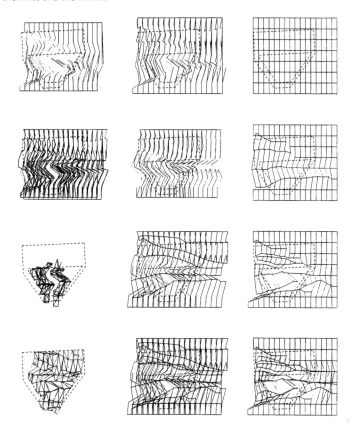

These pages: development of diagramatic models and contemporary evolution of design models.

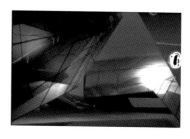

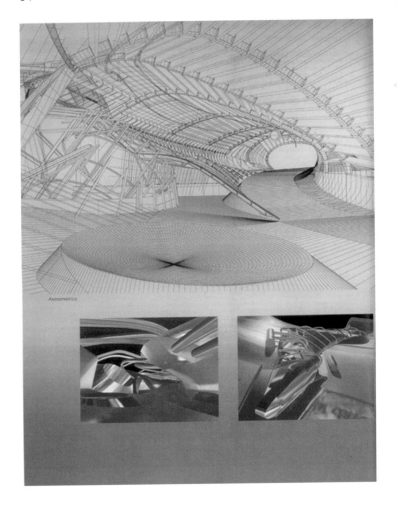

Axonometrics

Nox, Water Pavilion, *Neeltje Jans, Holland, 1994-97:* The fluid, silver-colored forms of the H2O pavilion seem to directly evoke the liquidity of water. The architectural design is based on the form of transformation. The conformation of the project originates from actions deforming fourteen different ellipses connected by radiating curves translated into lines of action and mutation; no section is ever the same as another. The customary distinction between the customary horizontal and vertical is lost in this building since the pavement blends in with the walls and the walls with the ceiling and the experience of walking is translated into a sensory as well as motor experience.

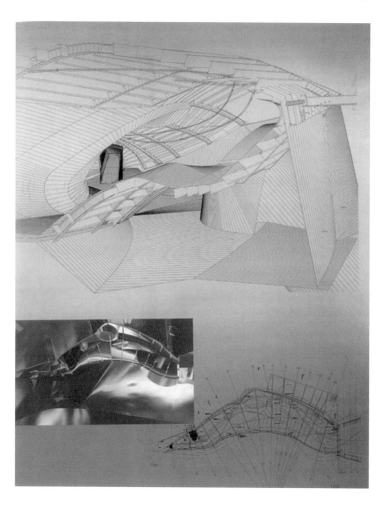

temporalities of animation software, augmented reality, computer-aided manufacture and informatics in general, topological "space" differs from Cartesian space in that it imbricates temporal events-within form. Space then, is no longer a vacuum within which subjects and objects are contained, space is instead transformed into an interconnected, dense web of particularities and singularities better understood as "substance" or "filled space". This nexus also entails more specifically the pervasive deployment

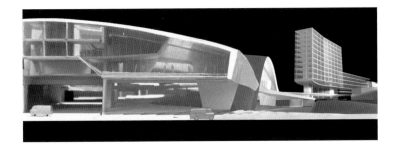

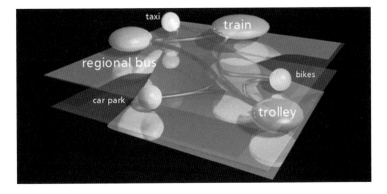

Ben van Berkel (UN Studio/van Berkel & Bos), Arnhem Central Station, Arnhem, 1996-2000. The new combination of intermodal exchange between various transport systems (trains, busses, taxis, parking areas, bicycles, etc.) is configured like an integrated whole of parts fluidly connected to one another, so that the architectural design seems to dissolve into the flows themselves of traffic movements. The heart of the construction is the double-high transfer hall, an empty space of interconnections that ties up the various types of pedestrian flows, condensing around it the continuous articulation of planes that curve and incline. The design process began with an analytical program of relationships between different transport systems, which shows a hierarchical relationship between the parts, and concludes with a unified architectural solution that takes its reference model from the geometric figure of the Klein Bottle.

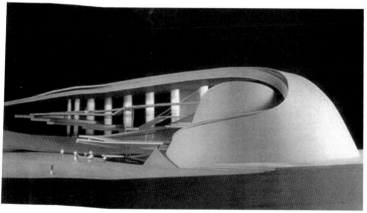

Anamorphosis Architects, Museum of the Hellenic World, Athens, 2002. Emphasis here is placed on the spatiality of the building that is shown as a great continuous space but diversified in its curves wrapped in the eye of a spiral. This nucleus was intended to symbolize the Ancient Period of Greek Civilization.

of teletechnology within praxis, leading to a usurping of the real (material) and an unintentional dependency on simulation.

Observations in which ideas flow together from geometry, topology, computer graphics, and space-time. The cultural links over the course of the years have functioned: new words, new meanings and new links.

Final Observations

I have attempted to report the most important moments leading to a change in our concept of perceiving space; presenting some key words that have marked this change; supplying some ideas and information; attempting to offer elements for reflection; to help reach beyond the technical and formal aspects although they are essential in mathematics; the cultural aspect of this brief history of the idea of space. Obviously I favored the geometric-mathematical aspect but always tried to keep in mind the intention of this book aimed at architects. I would just like to recall one or rather two greatly important final words: fantasy and liberty. These two magic words may have allowed contemporary architecture to greatly enrich the heritage of design. Fantasy and liberty that derive from the confluence of many elements over the course of the years. Those mentioned: the logic of the computer, new geometries, the fourth dimension, topology and computer graphics. Because even if only a few are aware of it, mathematics is, or can be, the realm of fantasy and liberty. In the hopes of belying that phrase from a poem by Rodari that says:

…and nothing remains any longer from all those many beautiful words.

Rodari was referring to the land of soap bubbles. The geometric structure of soap film has had and still has great importance in mathematics and architecture, but this is another story to be told another time.

Further Reading

These final pages furnish information and ideas for further study of some of the aspects mentioned in these pages. Being a mathematician, a lot of this information regards mathematics, but being a person who in the course of his life has also dealt professionally with cinema, art, exhibitions, and literature, in other words culture, many of these suggestions have been considered for a broad field of interests. First of all, there are some books that are my essential point of reference. For several years, I organized a conference at Ca' Foscari University in Venice on Mathematics and Culture. Several of the topics treated in this book have also been discussed there over the years.

On the links between mathematics and culture:

M. Emmer (ed.), *Matematica e cultura 1*, supplement to *Lettera Matematica*, Springer Verlag Italia, Milan 1998.

M. Emmer (ed.), *Matematica e cultura 2*, supplement to Lettera Matematica, Springer Verlag Italia, Milan 1999.

M. Emmer (ed.), *Matematica e cultura 2000*, Springer Verlag Italia, Milan 2000; Springer Verlag, Berlin 2003.

M. Emmer (ed.), *Matematica e cultura 2001*, Springer Verlag Italia, Milan 2001.

M. Emmer (ed.), *Matematica e cultura 2002*, Springer Verlag Italia, Milan 2002.

M. Emmer (ed.), *Matematica e cultura 2003*, with a music CD, Springer Verlag Italia, Milan 2003; Springer Verlag, Berlin 2003.

M. Emmer, M. Manaresi (eds.), *Matematica, arte, tecnologia, cinema*, Springer Verlag Italia, Milan 2002; 150 pages dedicated to cinema and mathematics; English edition Springer Verlag, Berlin 2003.

M. Emmer (ed.), *Matematica e Cultura 2004*, Springer Verlag Italia, Milan, to be printed March 2004.

Website of the congress *Matematica and cultura*: *http://www.mat.uniroma1.it/Venice 2004* (the date in October changes each year)

M. Kline, *Mathematics in Western Culture*, Oxford University Press, New York 1953. A book that has now become a classic written by a mathematics historian.

M. Kline, *mathematical Thought from Ancient to Modern Times*, Oxford University Press, New York 1990. The grand history of mathematics, not easy to read.

C. Boyer, *A History of mathematics*, Princeton University Press, Princeton 19785. An interesting history of mathematics that is also fairly easy to read.

F. Le Lionnais (ed.), *Les grands courants de la pensée mathématique*, Librairie Scientifique et Technique, A. Blanchard, Paris, 1962. See in particular the Le Corbusier article, *L'architecture et l'esprit mathématique*.

H. Poincaré, *La Science et L'hypothèse*, Flammarion, Paris 1968. Another classic, the reflections of a great mathematician.

D'Arcy W. Thompson, *On Growth and Form*, Cambridge University Press, Cambridge 1942. The first integrated attempt to mathematically explain the forms of nature.

The literature on fractal geometry is very broad. I will limit myself to citing:

B.B. Mandelbrot, *Fractals: Form, Chance and Dimension*, W.H. Freeman & Co., San Francisco, 1977. The book at the origin of it all.

H.O. Peitgen, P.H. Richter, *The Beauty of Fractals*, Springer-Verlag, Berlin 1986. The first and best book on geometry and fractal images.

From this book series La rivoluzione informatica (The Information Technology Revolution): A. Imperiale, *New Flatness*, Birkhäuser, Basel - Boston - Berlin 2001. The point of view of architects on many of the topics discussed here.

CHAPTER 2

J. Dieudonné, *Pour l'honneur de l'esprit humain*, Hachette, Paris 1987. Reflections of a great mathematician on mathematics.

R. Musil, *Man without Qualities*, volume I, A.A. Knopf, New York 1995.

R. Musil, *L'uomo matematico*, in *Sulla stupidità e altri scritti*, Mondadori, Milan 1986.

G.H. Hardy, *A Mathematician's Apology*, Cambridge University Press, New York 1940. A famous mathematician reflects on his life, mathematics, reality and art. When published, it received an excellent review from the famous writer G. Greene.

J.-P. Changeux, A. Connes, *Matière à pensée* , Odile Jacob, Paris, 1989. A famous neurobiologist and mathematician discuss the nature of mathematics.

R. Courant, H. Robbins, *What is Mathematics: An Elementary Approach to Idea and Methods*, Oxford University Press, New York 1941. For an idea of what mathematics is, this book is still unequaled after more than sixty years since its publication.

R. Osserman, *Poetry of the Universe*, Doubleday, New York 1995. A famous mathematician, called upon to teach a course on the origin of the universe to a class of very unmotivated students, writes a very beautiful book. Osserman is also responsible for the program *Lectures for the General Public* at the MSRI mathematical research center at Berkeley. Every year they create well-received videos, films or theatrical performances. The last one in 2003 was with Steve Martin and Robin Williams. Site: *http://www.msri.edu*.

CHAPTER 3

E.A. Abbott, Flatland: *A Romance of Many Dimensions by a Square*, Seeley & Co., London 1884.

M. Emmer, *Flatland*, film and video, 22 minutes, color, produced by Film 7 International, Rome 1994, Italian, French, English versions; for details see *http://www.mat.uniroma1.it/people/emmer*.

The Venice Biennale in 1986 was dedicated to the theme *Arte e Scienza* (*Arts and Sciences*); one section curated by Giulio Macchi was dedicated to the theme *Spazio* (*Space*). I curated a part of the section *Oltre la terza dimensione* (*Beyond the Third Dimension*) and some pages in the catalogue. G.Macchi (ed.), *Spazio*, catalogue of the section, Edizioni La Biennale, Venice 1986.

M.Emmer, *Dimensions*, film and video from the series "Art and Mathematics", produced by FILM 7, Rome (1987) color, 27 minutes, Italian, French and English versions. For details see *http://www.mat.uniroma1.it/people/emmer*.

A.S. Eddington, *Space, Time and Gravitation: An Outline of the General Relativity Theory*, Cambridge University Press, Cambridge 1920.

H.S.M. Coxeter, *Regular Polytopes*, Dover Publications Inc., New York 1973.

The bibliography on Dutch graphic artist Maurits Cornelis Escher is very broad. I will cite only books and films in which I have participated.

M. Emmer, D. Schattschneider (eds.), *M.C. Escher's Legacy*, Springer Verlag USA, New York 2003, with CD-ROM.

Book published on the hundredth anniversary of Escher's death.

H.S.M. Coxeter, M. Emmer, R. Penrose, M. Teuber (eds.), *Escher: Art and Science*, North-Holland, Amsterdam 1986. The first book in which the works of the Dutch graphic artist were studied from different points of view.

M. Emmer, *Il mondo fantastico di Escher*, video, 52 minutes, color, animation, produced by Film 7 International, 1996, versions in Italian, French, English, Spanish and Japanese. A film with animation and the participation of Escher's two mathematician friends: Roger Penrose and H.S. M. Coxeter.

Website and virtual Escher museum: *http://www.escherinhetpaleis.nl*.

L.H. Henderson, *The Fourth Dimension and Non-Euclidean Geometry in Modern Art*, Princeton University Press, Princeton (1983). The most important book on the relationship between mathematics, non-Euclidean geometry and Cubism and Futurism, debunking the myth of the awareness of Cubist painters of the theory of relativity. Out-of-print for years, it was reprinted in 2003 by MIT Press with a new introduction written by the author. Linda Henderson also appears in the above-mentioned video *Dimensioni*.

The publication De Stijl founded by Mondrian frequently published articles by mathematicians such as Poincaré or writings on mathematics. Here are two examples.

Th. van Doesburg, "Une nouvelle dimension pénétre notre conscience scientifique et plastique", in *De Stijl*, n. 2, 1927, pp. 21–22; anastatic reprint in *De Stijl*, vol. 2, 1921–1932, Athenaeum, Amsterdam 1968, pp. 538–539.

H. Poincaré, "Pourquoi l'espace a trois dimensions?", in *De Stijl*, no. 5, 1923, p. 66–70; anastatic reprint in *De Stijl*, vol. 2, 1921–1932, Athenaeum, Amsterdam 1968, pp. 377–379.

From the immense bibliography on the golden section I cite only:

Matila Ghika, *Le nombre d'or*, Gallimard, Paris 1931.

Matila Ghika, *Esthétique des Proportions dans la Nature et dans les arts*, Gallimard, Paris 1927. The last two books led to the rediscovery of the golden section in France. In particular, they influenced many of the choices of Le Modulor by Le Corbusier.

On the hypercube:

C. Strauss, T. Banchoff, *Hypercube*, film, 16 mm, computerized animation, 1978. This film was shown at the Venice Biennale in 1986 in the hall *Oltre la terza dimensione* (*Beyond the Third Dimension*).

T. Banchoff, *Oltre la terza dimensione*, Le Scienze Zanichelli, Bologna 1991. Banchoff website:

Hypercube, directed by Andrej Sekula.

A review of Hypercube and Cube: M. Emmer, "Hypercube and Cube", review, in *Bollettino Unione Matematica Italiana*, n. 8, VIA, April 2003, p. 183–190.

The articles by Novak and Perrella are reprinted in: G. Di Cristina (ed.), *Architecture and Science*, Wiley-Academy, London 2001.

CHAPTER 4

Among the innumerable editions of Swift's famous book, I recommend the following for their illustrations:

J. Swift, *Gulliver's Travel*, Bancroft, London 1966, with illustrations by Grandville, 1990.

Aside from the already cited: M. Kline, *Storia del pensiero matematico*, I recommend the following for understanding the history of the computer and formal logic:

U. Bottazzini, *Il Flauto di Hilbert*, UTET, Turin 2003.
For the story of Enigma and the life of Turing, the reference book is:
A. Hodges, *Storia di un Enigma*, Bollati Boringhieri, Turin 1991.
The Richard Harris novel, *Enigma*, is also interesting and was the basis for the film *Enigma* by Michael Apted, screenplay by Oscar winner Tom Stoppard. This film is mentioned in the English edition of the book: M. Emmer, M. Manaresi, Mathematics, *Art, Technology and Cinema* cit.

CHAPTER 5

Aside from the already mentioned book by Courant and Robbins, another popular mathematical classic is:
D. Hilbert, S. Cohn-Vossen, *Geometria intuitiva*, Bollati Boringhieri, Turin 2001. An appendix at the end of this book contains a long article by Russian mathematician Alexandrov on the fundamentals of topology.
See also this book on the relationship between mathematics and art, in particular topology and art:
M. Emmer, *L'occhio di Horus: itinerari nell'immaginario matematico*, Istituto della Enciclopedia Italiana, Rome, 1989. At present this book can only be found in libraries. In 1989, I organized a large traveling exhibit of the same title on the theme of mathematics and art. The exhibit toured Bologna, Parma, Milan and Rome and was visited by thousands of people. RAI filmed it as a documentary in the series, "Le grandi mostre dell'anno" ("The Year's Great Exhibits"). Part of the exhibit and book were dedicated to topology.
On the Möbius Strip in art and mathematics, see:
M. Emmer, *Il nastro di Möbius*, film and video, 27 minutes, color, 1984; Max Bill appears in the film to speak about its surfaces with only one side.
Again on the relationship between mathematics, art and computer graphics see:
M. Emmer (ed.), *The Visual Mind*, The MIT Press, Boston 1993. The cover reproduces a piece by Max Bill and an article appears in the book written by Bill in 1949 on the relationship between mathematics and art, with several corrections by the author.
A new volume will be released in 2004:
M. Emmer (ed.), *The Visual Mind 2*, The MIT Press, Boston.
See also the catalogue of the large Max Bill exhibit at the Palazzo della Pilotta in Parma: A. Quintavalle, *Max Bill*, Quaderni n. 38, Dipartimento di Arte Contemporanea, Università di Parma, 1977.
On architecture and topology, see the doctoral thesis, for which I was one of the examiners, by Giuseppa Di Cristina, published in 1999: G. Di Cristina, *Architettura e topologia: per una teoria spaziale dell'architettura*, Editrice Librerie Dedalo, Rome.
And especially the richly illustrated volume with articles by the most interesting architects who have worked with this topic: G. Di Cristina (ed.), *Architecture and Science*, Wiley-Academy, London 2001.

ADDITIONAL BIBLIOGRAPHY
by Giuseppa Di Cristina

Topology and Morphogenesis, Ed. La Biennale, Venice 1978.
P. Eisenman, *La fine del classico*, Cluva, Venice 1987.

P. Eisenman, "Oltre lo sguardo. L'architettura nell'epoca dei media elettronici", in *Domus*, no. 734, January 1992.

Architectural Design, Vol. 63 no. 3-4, 1993 (*Folding in Architecture*).

M. Wigley, *The Architecture of Deconstruction, Derrida's Haunt*, The MIT Press, Cambridge 1993.

B. van Berkel, *Mobile Forces / Mobile Kräfte*, Ernst & Sohn Verlag, Berlin 1994.

G. Schmitt, *Architectura et Machina*, Vieweg, Wiesbaden 1993.

J. Frazer, *An Evolutionary Architecture*, Architectural Association, London 1995.

Ch. Jencks, *The Architecture of the Jumping Universe. A Polemic*, Academy Editions, London 1995.

Hani Rashid + Lise Anne Couture, *Architecture for the Future*, Asymptote Architecture, Pierre Terrail Editions, Paris 1996.

B. Tschumi, *Architecture and Disjunction*, The MIT Press, Cambridge 1996.

A.L. Huxtable, *The Unreal America: Architecture and Illusion*, The New Press, New York 1997.

J. Beckmann (ed.), *The Virtual Dimension: Architecture, Representation, and Crash Culture*, Princeton Architectural Press, New York 1998.

G. Lynn, *Folds, bodies & blobs. Collected Essays*, La lettre volée, Paris 1998.

G. Lynn, *Animate Form*, Princeton Architectural Press, New York 1999.

Hani Rashid + Lise Anne Couture, *Asymptote Flux*, Phaidon, London 2002.

The Information Technology Revolution in Architecture is a new series reflecting on the effects the virtual dimension is having on architects and architecture in general. Each volume will examine a single topic, highlighting the essential aspects and exploring their relevance for the architects of today.

Other titles in this series: